SimEarth

THE LIVING PLANET™

USER MANUAL

SimEarth User Manual by
MICHAEL BREMER

SimEarth Credits
Concept and Design: Will Wright and Fred Haslam

Design Assistance: James Lovelock

Macintosh Programming: Fred Haslam, Will Wright
IBM Programming: Daniel Goldman, Paul Schmidt
Windows Programming: Rodney T. Lai, Paul Schmidt
Computer Graphics: Peter & Caitlin Mitchell-Dayton,
Jenny Martin, Suzie Greene
Macintosh Sound and Music: Steve Hales
IBM Sound and Music: Heath Paterson

Package Design: Richard Bagel, Kurt West
Package Illustration: Kurt West
Documentation Design: Richard Bagel, Kurt West,
Chris Yoro, Mark Holmes, Michael Bremer

Documentation: Michael Bremer
Introduction to Earth Science: Carolina Lithgow,
Tom Bentley
Contributions to Documentation: James Lovelock,
Will Wright, Fred Haslam, Tom Bentley,
Robin Samelson, Michael Patterson, Bill Cook,
Joe Scirica

Product Managers: Steve Beckert, IBM & Mac
Mitzi S. McGilvray, Windows
King of Manufacturing: Dave Helfenstein
Q/A & Tech Support: Bill Cook, Steve Smythe, Alan Barton,
Manny J. Granillo, Jake Hoelter, Kevin O'Hare,
Michael Patterson, Carter Lipscomb

Special Thanks to: Jeff Braun, Stewart Brand, Eric Albers,
David Anderson, Brian Rosborough, Kimberly Schmidt,
Janice Linden-Reed, Morris Meislik, Michael Clapp,
Chris Crawford, James Kalin, and Brøderbund Software.

Testers: Kara Alber, Eric Albers, Chris Allen, Harvey Lee,
Steve Beckert, Jeff Braun, Michael Bremer, Bill Cook,
Daniel Goldman, Ann & Don Goldman, Jake Hoelter,
James Kalin, Scott Kim, Janice Linden-Reed,
James Lovelock, Bob Mandel, Michael Patterson, Robin
Samelson, Paul Schmidt, Chris Weiss, and Corey Nelson
and the team at Testing 1,2,3...

**Dedicated to Gaia, without whom this game would not
be possible.**

MAXIS Two Theatre Square, Suite 230
Orinda, CA 94563-3041
510 254-9700   FAX: 510 253-3736

IBM Version   ISBN # 0-929750-32-2
Macintosh Version ISBN # 0-929750-33-0
Windows Version   ISBN # 0-929750-46-2

Limited Warranty
The SimEarth program and documentation are provided "as
is" without warranty of any kind. Maxis warrants to the
original purchaser of SimEarth that the diskette will be free
from defects in materials and workmanship for ninety days
from the date of purchase. Maxis reserves the right to make
improvements in the product described in this manual at any
time and without notice.

Replacement of Media
SimEarth has no disk-based copy protection. You are free to
make backup copies for personal use. Defective media
returned within ninety days from date of purchase will be
replaced without charge. Returning the registration card will
extend the warranty.

License
As the original purchaser, you have the right to use SimEarth
only on a single computer. You may physically transfer the
program from one computer to another provided the
program is used only on one computer at any time. You may
not distribute copies of SimEarth or accompanying
documentation to others.

SIMEARTH CONTENTS

INTRODUCTION

"Is this a random world or did you
planet?"

*The most pondered question by SimEarthling
philosophers.*

SimEarth

WHAT IS SIMEARTH?

SimEarth is a planet simulator—a model of a planet. It is a game, an educational toy, and an enjoyable tool. With SimEarth you can take over many included planets, or design and create your own.

SimEarth is based on the Gaia theory by James Lovelock, which suggests that we look at our planet and the life on it as a whole, and not as separate areas of study.

SimEarth treats the planet as a whole: life, climate, the atmosphere, and the planet itself—from dirt and rock to the molten core—all affect each other.

You will see your planet as a whole—from a satellite's point of view, at two levels of magnification.

SimEarth can be played in two modes: *game* and *experimental*. In game mode, you will try to develop, manage, and preserve your planet within allotted energy budgets.

In experimental mode, you are given unlimited energy to mold your planet. This allows you to set up any type of planet in any stage of development, and then introduce any new factors you want and see what happens. In this mode SimEarth is a "planetary spreadsheet."

Your SimEarth planets will be populated by electronic life-forms called SimEarthlings—cousins of the Sims who populate SimCity™ (another fine product from Maxis). SimEarthlings range from single-celled plants and animals to intelligent species.

Intelligent SimEarthlings are not limited to Humans—or even Mammals. There can be intelligent Dinosaur SimEarthlings, intelligent Mollusk SimEarthlings, even intelligent Insect SimEarthlings—but only one intelligent life-form at a time.

A single planet can be populated by billions and billions of SimEarthlings. Their welfare is in your hands.

WHAT IS GAIA?

by JAMES LOVELOCK,
the originator of the Gaia theory

Gaia is a theory about the evolution of the Earth. A theory that sees the evolution of the species of organisms by natural selection and the evolution of the rocks, air and oceans as a single tightly coupled process. In Gaia the organisms and their material environment together constitute a system which is able to self-regulate climate and atmospheric composition.

The fact that the Earth's mean temperature has remained constant and favourable for life for 3.6 billion years in spite of a rise in output of heat from the Sun of 25%, and the fact that oxygen has remained close to 21% of our atmosphere for 200 million years, can be explained by Gaia theory but not by conventional science. Although it is a scientific theory, the name Gaia was proposed by the novelist William Golding.

Gaia became visible through the new knowledge about the Earth gained from space and from the extensive investigations of the Earth's surface, oceans and atmosphere during the past few decades. This view has in it something of the poetic metaphor of a ship held by the sailors, but it is also a hard science theory of our planet that came from a top-down view from space. This theory is now up for trial, and the evidence gathered from the Earth itself will decide on whether or not it should be taken as scientific fact. Don't be misled by those who argue that Gaia is untestable or teleological and therefore in error; their criticism is mere opinion based on prejudice, not evidence. Even if in the end Gaia should turn out to be no more than a poetic metaphor, it would still have been worth thinking of the Earth as a living system. Such thoughts have already led to discoveries about the Earth that could not have come from conventional wisdom.

Gaia is a top-down view of the Earth as a single system, and is essentially physiological. It is about the working of the whole system, not with the separated parts of a planet divided arbitrarily into the biosphere, the atmosphere, the lithosphere and the hydrosphere. These are not real divisions of the Earth; they are spheres of influence inhabited by academic scientists.

All I ask is that you concede that there might be something in the Gaia theory, which sees the Earth as a living system, to acknowledge Gaia at least for the purpose of argument. I do not expect you to become converts to a new Earth religion. I do not ask you to suspend your common sense. All that I do ask is that you consider Gaia theory as an alternative to the conventional wisdom of a dead planet made of inanimate rocks, ocean and atmosphere merely inhabited by life. Consider it as a real system, comprising all of life and all of its environment tightly coupled so as to form a self-regulating entity. Maybe you already have it in mind

when you use that vague, ill-defined word "Biosphere" that seems to have a different meaning for each occasion of its use.

I recognise that to view the Earth as if it were alive is just a convenient, but different, way of organising the facts of the Earth. I am of course prejudiced in favor of Gaia and have filled my life for the past 25 years with the thought that Earth may be alive: not as the ancients saw her—a sentient Goddess with a purpose and foresight—but alive like a tree. A tree that quietly exists, never moving except to sway in the wind, yet endlessly conversing with the sunlight and the soil. Using sunlight and water and nutrient minerals to grow and change. But all done so imperceptibly, that to me the old oak tree on the green is the same as it was when I was a child.

SOFTWARE TOYS AND SYSTEM SIMULATIONS

SOFTWARE TOYS

SimEarth isn't exactly a game...it's what we call a "Software Toy." Toys, by definition, are more flexible and open-ended than games.

As an example, compare a game, tennis, with a toy, a ball. In every tennis game, there is one way to begin, one goal to pursue, and one way to end. There are infinite variations in the middle, but they all start the same way, chase the same goal, and end the same way.

A ball is more flexible—there are more things you can do with it. With the ball, you can play tennis. You can play catch. You can throw it at someone. You can bounce it. You can make up a hundred different games using the ball.

Our Software Toys are programmable. Using the comparison with a ball, this means that you can change the tennis ball into a football, baseball, soccer ball, Ping Pong ball, etc., and play any and all the games you play with those balls.

Besides games, there are other things you can do with a ball. You can paint it, use it to plug a leaky roof, or just contemplate its roundness.

In SimEarth, the "toy" is a planet—a programmable planet that can become an infinite number of planets.

So when you play with SimEarth, or any of our Software Toys, don't limit yourself to trying to "win." Play with it. Experiment. Try new things. Just have fun.

SYSTEM SIMULATIONS

There are many types of toys. SimEarth, like SimCity before it, is a SYSTEM SIMULATION toy. In a system simulation, we provide you with a set of RULES and TOOLS that describe, create and control a system. In the case of SimEarth, the system is a planet.

Part of the challenge of playing with a SYSTEM SIMULATION toy is to figure out how the system works and take control of it. As master of the system you are free to use the TOOLS to create and control an unlimited number of systems (in this case, planets) within the framework provided by the RULES.

In SimEarth, the RULES to learn are based on global systems and management, including:

Chemical Factors:	atmospheric composition, energy management
Geological Factors:	climate, extraterrestrial collisions, continental drift, earthquakes
Biological Factors:	formation of life, evolution, food supply, biome types and distribution
Human Factors:	wars, civilization, technology, waste control, pollution, food supply, energy supply

The TOOLS provide you with the ability to create, modify and manage a planet:
Create a planet in any of four Time Scales.
Physically modify the landscape of the planet.
Set the altitude of any spot on the planet.
Trigger events on the planet from hurricanes to volcanos to meteor strikes.
Plant various biomes and life-forms anywhere on the planet.
Nurture a species to help it evolve intelligence.
Manage your planet by making use of the available maps and graphs.

But the most important TOOL of all is the simulator itself. Test your plans, theories and ideas as you watch your planet develop or decline. Customize the simulation by changing the rules that control the geosphere, the atmosphere, the biosphere, and civilization, to suit yourself or test life's adaptability to various conditions.

SIMULATION LIMITATIONS AND BIASES

SIMULATION LIMITATIONS

Anything as complicated as the Earth or an animal or even a city cannot be completely defined by formulas and equations. Any model of something this complicated cannot be completely accurate—but if you are aware of the inaccuracies, the model can still be useful.

A street map is a model of a city. It isn't a completely accurate representation of every detail of a city, but, within its limitations, it's very useful. Most of us would be lost without one.

As a simulation of a real planetary system, SimEarth is a rough caricature—an extreme simplification. We simulate many different aspects of a planet, including climate, evolution, atmospheric composition, and civilization, all on a personal computer.

A truly accurate simulation for a climate model alone has not yet been realized even on today's most powerful super-computers. We designed this simulation as accurately as we could while maintaining compatibility with personal computers and including a gaming aspect.

A major limitation to this program is how evolution is treated. It closely follows Earth's evolution. With very few exceptions, all the life-forms represented here actually exist or existed on Earth. While allowing many differences in which species succeed or fail—and eventually gain sentience—the path from single-celled life to complex life is roughly the same as on Earth.

Also, whatever species becomes intelligent—Mammal, Dinosaur, Fish, etc.—will develop civilizations, cities and technologies that greatly resemble Human civilizations, cities and technologies.

BIASES

SimEarth is based on the Gaia theory, as proposed by James Lovelock. Gaia theory is controversial, and not an accepted truth in all scientific circles.

For this game, we are also making a few assumptions that are not necessarily true. One of these assumptions is that intelligence is an evolutionary advantage—we might just be flattering ourselves.

The simulator in SimEarth is a very complex piece of modeling software. It is constantly performing many checks, calculations and updates, as well as keeping watch on the mouse and keyboard to respond to your demands.

When you load in a planet, give the simulator a minute or two to compile and update maps and graphs.

When you make adjustments to the MODEL CONTROL PANELS, allow some time for the changes to take effect.

Simulator reaction time is also greatly affected by your computer's clock speed and type of microprocessor.

SCENARIOS

Each of the seven included scenario planets is actually a game in itself that can be played at three levels of difficulty or in experimental mode. Each scenario will present you with different challenges in planet management.

TESTING THE GAIA HYPOTHESIS— DAISYWORLD

One of the main tenets of the Gaia hypothesis is that life itself regulates the conditions on Earth that support life, including temperature and atmospheric content.

One of the scenarios, Daisyworld, is a simplified simulation with only eight life-forms: differently shaded daisies. This scenario is based on the original Daisyworld computer model James Lovelock designed to explain the Gaia hypothesis.

Experimenting with the Daisyworld Scenario will give you a visual demonstration of the concept of Gaia and of life on Earth as a self-regulating whole.

A complete description of how and why the Daisyworld model works is found later in this manual, in the "Scenarios" chapter.

TAKING ON THE ROLE OF GAIA

If you play any of the scenarios or random planets at the most difficult level, all Gaian self-regulation will be disabled. You will have to constantly monitor and adjust everything on the planet to keep life in existence.

SIMULATOR REACTION TIME

GOALS OF SIMEARTH

YOUR OWN PLANETS

Besides the scenarios, you can create an unlimited number of different planets, at various levels of difficulty.

FUN AND CHALLENGE

Running a planet is a real challenge for even an experienced gamer.

OTHER GOALS

Design, modify, manage, and nurture a planet from creation through formation of the oceans, to the appearance of life, through the evolution of life, through the development of intelligence and technology, to the point where your SimEarthlings can reach for the stars.

Set up a planetary situation and just watch what happens.

Choose and help a particular species gain mastery of the planet.

Influence the life to keep it from destroying itself and the planet.

Perhaps the ultimate goal of SimEarth is for you to design, manage and maintain the planet of your dreams. Your ideal planet may be a high-tech society of intelligent humans (or intelligent dinosaurs) or a limited-technology planet where the biosphere is never endangered.

YOUR OWN GOALS

It's your toy—you make the rules. You don't need a goal if you don't want one. Just play.

ABOUT THIS MANUAL

This manual has two functions: to teach you how to use SimEarth and to introduce you to the basics of Earth Science.

The majority of this manual describes the program *SimEarth*: how it works, how to use it, how it deals with life, climate, geology, atmospheric composition, civilization, etc.

The Introduction to Earth Science section of this manual deals with many of the same things as they are in the real world, out of the context of SimEarth.

This manual covers the SimEarth program for all computers. Any machine-specific information for installing, starting, or using SimEarth will be found on the included system card/addendum.

The graphics used in this manual are taken from the Macintosh monochrome and IBM Hercules and MCGA monochrome versions of SimEarth. Depending on your computer and monitor type, the graphics you see on your screen may vary slightly.

In SimEarth there are two uses of energy. You, the player, use it to make, mold, modify and manipulate the planet, and civilized SimEarthlings make and use it to carry on their daily lives. A complete explanation of energy and its uses in SimEarth is found in the "Energy" chapter of this manual.

ABOUT ENERGY

SIMEARTHLING USE OF ENERGY

Intelligent SimEarthlings will produce and use energy. You can control their choice of energy sources and their use of the energy they produce, but you don't have *direct* access to *their* energy for *your* purposes.

YOUR USE OF ENERGY

Depending on the difficulty level of the game, you will have different amounts of energy to affect the planet and the simulation. These amounts are both your starting supply and the maximum you can accumulate at any one time.

If you are in experimental mode, you will have an unlimited supply of energy.

Energy for a game comes from the stores of the planet itself in the form of geothermal, wind, and solar energy, as well as fossil fuels. As you deplete your energy supplies during a game, they will slowly build back up over time as the planet increases its energy from the above sources. This continual tapping of the planet's energies happens automatically.

Once life on your planet becomes intelligent, you will automatically tap some of their energy. You can't just take the energy: a certain amount will be added to your supply along with the energy tapped from the planet itself.

The higher the level of technology on your planet, the more energy you will receive.

BLANK PAGE

GETTING STARTED

"All the world's a simulation
And all the Sims and SimEarthlings merely players..."

William Simspeare

SimEarth

INSTALLING SIMEARTH

Please refer to the enclosed system card and machine-specific addendum for installation instructions.

GETTING HELP

SimEarth is a fairly complex program, with lots of windows, icons, buttons, options, and control panels. To make your simulating experience easier, there is a lot of help information included in the program.

HELP

THE HELP FUNCTION
Any time you want or need help, or aren't sure what something in the program does, ask for help. Whenever you hold down the SHIFT KEY, you are in help mode, and the cursor changes to ▲HELP. Then click on anything anywhere in SimEarth, and you will get a help message.

THE GLOSSARY
There is an on-line glossary that defines many of the words in the SimEarth program.

To access the glossary, open the WINDOWS MENU, and select GLOSSARY.

There is also a Glossary in the Appendix section of this manual.

THE TUTORIALS
There is a tutorial section in this manual. There is also an on-line abbreviated version of the tutorial.

The on-line text-based tutorial is accessed by selecting TUTORIAL from the WINDOWS MENU. You can even keep the TUTORIAL WINDOW open on the screen while playing the game, and refer to it whenever you need.

Depending on your computer, you may or may not be able to have the on-line tutorial open at the same time as other HELP WINDOWS.

STARTING THE PROGRAM

Please refer to the system card or machine-specific addendum for instructions in starting SimEarth.

The first time you start the program, you will see three windows: the TITLE WINDOW, which goes away as soon as you click the mouse, the EDIT WINDOW, which is your main planetary work space, and a HELP WINDOW, which will tell you how to get started and how to get more help.

Whenever you start SimEarth, there will be no active planet. You will have to select either NEW PLANET or LOAD PLANET from the FILE MENU before the simulation will really start. This is to give you a chance to look around, play with the various windows and controls, and prepare yourself before things start to happen.

The following Tutorial section will guide you through the basics of planet creation and manipulation.

SimEarth

ANOTHER BLANK PAGE

TUTORIAL

SimEarth

"Fools make a mock at Sim."

SimProverbs xiv. 9.

INTRODUCTION

The purpose of this tutorial is to give you a quick tour of SimEarth's menus, windows, and planet manipulation tools. It won't give every detail of every item in the program. For in-depth explanations of everything in the program see the Reference section of this manual.

BASIC CONCEPTS

Before beginning the tutorial, here are a few basic concepts and terms to get you started.

GAIA THEORY

SimEarth is based on the Gaia theory. Everything in the program is interrelated: climate, animals, plants, and the planet itself all affect each other.

A brief explanation of the Gaia theory is given in the Introduction in the chapter "What is Gaia?" A demonstration of how Gaia works is found in the Daisyworld section of the "Scenarios" chapter.

PLANET

The term "planet" refers to the present planet, world, or scenario that is loaded into memory and is being simulated.

You will view your planet from a satellite's point of view at two different magnifications, and as either a flat robinson projection or a globe.

SIMULATION/SIMULATOR

In SimEarth and this manual, we use the terms "simulation" and "simulator" to represent the part of the program that is modelling the planet. When you change or modify the simulation, you are changing variables and parameters in the model, which in turn change the planet.

The ability to modify the simulation is a powerful tool both for the gaming aspect and the experimental "planetary spreadsheet" aspect of SimEarth.

INPUT AND OUTPUT

SimEarth is a very complicated program. An important part of understanding it is knowing where you can INPUT (change the planet or simulation), and where you find OUTPUT (results of your INPUT).

There are three places for INPUT:
The FILE MENU for creating or loading planets;
The EDIT WINDOW for making local changes to spots on the planet; and
The MODEL CONTROL PANELS for modifying the simulation and changing the planet globally.

The MODEL CONTROL PANELS are the only places in SimEarth that are INPUT only.

Everything else—all the maps and graphs, even the EDIT WINDOW—supplies OUTPUT.

TIME LIMIT

In SimEarth, as on the real Earth, the level of solar radiation is continually increasing. You only have 10 billion years before the planet gets so hot that all life on it will die.

Technically, the Sun cools off as it expands into a red giant. As it expands, it gets closer to the planet. From the planet's position, the solar radiation is increasing even though the Sun is cooling.

TIME SCALES

There are four Time Scales in SimEarth: Geologic, Evolution, Civilized, and Technology. Each Time Scale simulates different periods of a planet's development at different rates of speed.

You can begin a planet in any Time Scale, or start at the first (Geologic) and guide your planet through them all. A certain amount of development must occur before advancing to the next one.

BIOMES

Biomes are ecological systems of plants and animals, such as Forest, Desert and Jungle. Where a particular biome can survive depends on temperature, rainfall and altitude. For the most part, biomes are used in SimEarth to represent the plant life of a planet.

LIFE

Life-forms in SimEarth (SimEarthlings) range from single-celled microbes in the ocean to complex, intelligent animals. Any multicellular life-form in SimEarth can become intelligent.

Life will begin and evolve automatically in SimEarth. To a great extent, you can affect the evolutionary path that life follows on your planet.

There are 15 classes of life represented in SimEarth. Each class of life has 16 species. There are 240 possible forms of life, but not all of them will develop or survive on any given planet.

The symbols that represent life in the EDIT WINDOW stand for a large population of that life-form—not just one animal.

Each form of life has favorite biomes where it flourishes, and others where it cannot survive at all.

The level of development of life controls the advancement of Time Scales.

CIVILIZATION

Eventually, one type of SimEarthling will attain sentience. When this happens, civilization begins. With civilization comes many new issues and problems to deal with.

SimEarth simulates civilization with cities at seven levels of technology ranging from the Stone Age of the distant past to the Nanotech Age of the future.

ENERGY

There are two uses of energy in SimEarth: yours and the SimEarthlings.

You use energy each time you change the planet in the EDIT WINDOW or the MODEL CONTROL PANELS. Creating and nurturing your planet within your energy budget is one of the challenges of SimEarth.

Intelligent SimEarthlings produce and use energy. You can control their energy production and use, but it's theirs—you can't use their energy for planet manipulation.

HELP AND THE GLOSSARY

On-line help is available anywhere at any time in SimEarth. To access help, hold down the SHIFT KEY and click somewhere on the screen. A text window will appear with the information you need.

One special use of the HELP WINDOW is the GLOSSARY. There may be some words that you don't know in this program. If you choose GLOSSARY from the WINDOWS MENU, a glossary of the words and terms used in this program will appear in the HELP WINDOW.

This tutorial will be presented in three sections:

FIRST LOOK will introduce you to the various menus, windows, graphs, and control panels.

CREATING AND MODIFYING PLANETS will teach you how to create and save planets; change the landform of a planet; place and move biomes, life and cities on a planet; and trigger events such as volcanos and earthquakes.

MODIFYING THE SIMULATION shows how you can use the MODEL CONTROL PANELS to change global conditions on your planet.

ABOUT THIS TUTORIAL

FIRST LOOK

See the system card and addendum for your machine for installation and startup instructions, and fire it up.

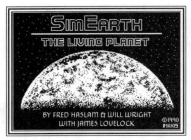

You will see a MENU BAR across the top of the screen, plus three separate windows: a TITLE SCREEN, a HELP WINDOW, and the MAP WINDOW.

The TITLE SCREEN introduces the program and gives credits. Click on it to make it go away.

The HELP WINDOW holds text that will help you use and understand SimEarth. You can request help on any icon, any button, any window, any function, any anything in SimEarth.

The first time you start the program, the HELP WINDOW will display text to help you get started.

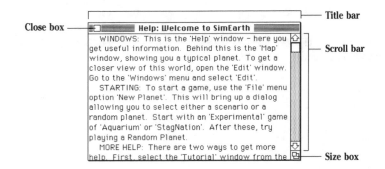

You can change the size of the HELP WINDOW by clicking and dragging the SIZE BOX. You can move it around the screen by clicking and dragging the TITLE BAR.

To scroll through all the text in a HELP WINDOW click on the up or down arrows in the SCROLL BAR on the right side of the window.

To make the HELP WINDOW go away, click in the CLOSE BOX.

The MAP WINDOW gives you a view of your entire planet.

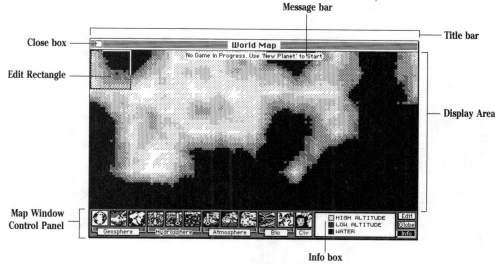

Message bar

Title bar

Close box —

Edit Rectangle —

Display Area

Map Window
Control Panel

Info box

At the top of the MAP WINDOW is the TITLE BAR. It displays the name of the current map display. You can move the MAP WINDOW around the screen by clicking and dragging the TITLE BAR. At the left of the TITLE BAR is the CLOSE BOX. If you click in this box the MAP WINDOW will close. To bring it back, select MAP from the WINDOWS MENU.

All windows, graphs and control panels have TITLE BARS and CLOSE BOXES.

The MAP WINDOW also has a DISPLAY AREA and a CONTROL PANEL. The DISPLAY AREA shows the entire planet. A rectangle somewhere in this area shows the part of the planet that will be displayed in the EDIT WINDOW, your close-up view of the planet.

The CONTROL PANEL, at the bottom of the window, lets you select different views of the planet that give you information about the land, water, air, climate, life and civilization. The views are changed by clicking on the 12 icons. Go ahead and click on them. Many of them won't do much because there is no active planet. To get the original view back, click on the far left icon.

Clicking on the little buttons at the bottom that say GEOSPHERE, ATMOSPHERE, BIO, and CIV will bring up various MODEL CONTROL PANELS, and double-clicking on some of the icons will bring up graphs. Don't worry about this now. If an unexpected small window pops up, close it by clicking in its CLOSE BOX, or just click on any part of the MAP WINDOW to bring it to the front.

Near the right side of the CONTROL PANEL is the INFO BOX. It displays various graphs and legends for each of the map views. To the right of the INFO BOX are three buttons. The top one takes you to the EDIT WINDOW; the bottom one changes the INFO BOX between graphs and legends (when available).

The middle button, GLOBE, changes the flat map into a globe. All of the map views are available on both the flat map and the globe. Click on GLOBE again to return to the flat map.

At the top of the DISPLAY AREA is a MESSAGE BAR that will sometimes appear and display messages to you from the simulation and from the SimEarthlings that inhabit the planet.

At the moment, the MESSAGE BAR should say, "No Game in Progress. Use 'New Planet' to Start." When SimEarth first starts, there is no actual planet or game running. This gives you a chance to look around a little before things start to happen. When you are ready to start playing, you must choose NEW PLANET from the FILE MENU.

Before doing that, we'll take a quick look around.

Look at the MENUS along the top of the screen. If you are unfamiliar with drop-down menus, check with the SimEarth addendum for your machine. A complete description of every item on every menu is found in the Reference section of this manual.

Open the FILE MENU. It is for starting new planets, loading and saving old planets, printing, and quitting SimEarth.

Open the WINDOWS MENU. Use this menu to open the various SimEarth windows.

Open the MODELS MENU. This menu gives you access to the four MODEL CONTROL PANELS that you will use to modify the simulation.

Open the GRAPHS MENU. This menu gives you access to the four graphs that give you information on air, life and technology on the planet.

Open the OPTIONS MENU. It lets you customize the program to your tastes.

Open the SPEED MENU. It lets you set the simulation speed of the game and choose the way the date is displayed.

Open the DATASOUND MENU. It lets you control some of the sound in SimEarth.

Along with the MAP WINDOW, the most important window you will be using is the EDIT WINDOW. To see it, choose EDIT from the WINDOWS MENU. For a complete description of everything in the EDIT WINDOW, see the Reference section of this manual. Here's a once-over.

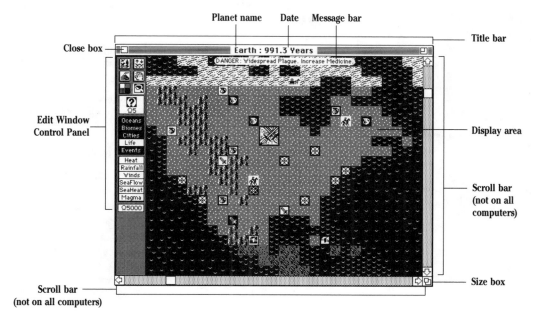

The EDIT WINDOW is your close-up view of your planet. It is where you will make modifications to the planet itself and the life on it.

The EDIT WINDOW also has a TITLE BAR, CONTROL PANEL, and a DISPLAY AREA. You can use the TITLE BAR to close or move the window. The DISPLAY AREA shows the area of the planet that is in the rectangle in the MAP WINDOW.

Edit Window Control Panel

On the left side of the window is the EDIT WINDOW CONTROL PANEL. This is where you choose your tools to modify the planet, and choose the data you want to view in this window.

An easy way to find out what all the icons and buttons on the EDIT WINDOW CONTROL PANEL do is to use the HELP function. Hold down the SHIFT KEY and click on an icon or button. The HELP WINDOW will give you information on the spot where you clicked.

In the lower-right corner is the SIZE BOX. Click and drag this box to enlarge or shrink the size of the EDIT WINDOW.

The biggest part of this window is the DISPLAY AREA. This is the close-up "satellite's eye view" of your planet. At this point you will see only land and water in this area. The elevation of the land is shown in shades—the lighter the shade, the higher the elevation.

To see different parts of the planet you must scroll the planet's terrain under the window. Depending on your computer, you may or may not have SCROLL BARS at the right and bottom of the EDIT WINDOW. If you have SCROLL BARS, then use them (click on the arrows or the bar) to scroll the terrain. If you don't have SCROLL BARS, then simply move the mouse pointer to any edge or corner of the screen, and the display will scroll.

Go to the WINDOWS MENU and open the TUTORIAL WINDOW. This is a HELP WINDOW that introduces you to SimEarth and explains much of the program. The tutorial that you are reading now is much more complete. Use the on-line TUTORIAL WINDOW for a quick refresher course whenever you need it.

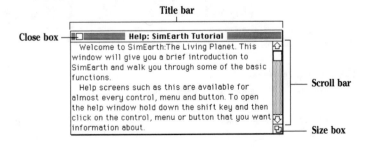

There is also a HISTORY WINDOW that graphs 15 factors through the history of your planet, and a REPORT WINDOW, which gives you feedback on your planet's condition and your planet management skills. Since there is no active planet yet, these windows won't tell you much. We'll come back to them later.

Open the MODELS MENU and select GEOSPHERE. You will see the GEOSPHERE MODEL CONTROL PANEL. Go back to the menu and select ATMOSPHERE to see another CONTROL PANEL.

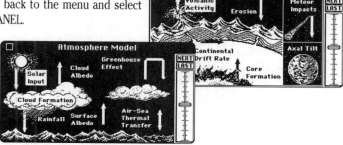

These CONTROL PANELS, four in all, let you modify the actual simulation. You can only display one MODEL CONTROL PANEL at a time. You can switch between them by clicking on the NEXT or LAST buttons in the upper-right corner of the panel.

Open the GRAPHS MENU and select one of the graphs. Only one graph can be viewed at a time. These graphs keep you informed on the status of the Atmosphere, Biomes, Life, and Technology on your planet.

Let's build some planets.

CREATING AND MODIFYING PLANETS
CREATING A PLANET IN THE GEOLOGIC TIME SCALE

Select NEW PLANET from the FILE MENU.

You will see the NEW PLANET WINDOW.

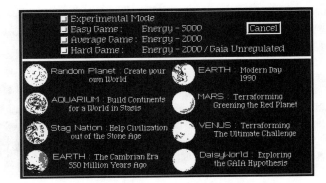

At the top of this window, you select whether you want to play an easy, average, or hard game. You can also select experimental mode, which gives you an unlimited energy budget.

The bottom of the window gives you choices of planets. There are seven scenarios—pre-set planets—that you can load, or you can create a random planet.

Let's create a random planet in easy game mode. Click on EASY GAME in the top section of the window, and click on the planet that says RANDOM PLANET.

Now you will see a dialog box asking you to name your planet and select the Time Scale.

There are four Time Scales in SimEarth; each simulates different aspects of planetary development. There is a complete description of each Time Scale in the Reference section.

Click in the box next to GEOLOGIC (it may already be selected), then type in a name for your planet—try GEOWORLD—and click the BEGIN button.

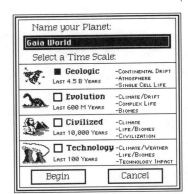

A new planet is born. Select the EDIT option in the WINDOWS MENU and look at the EDIT WINDOW. In the TITLE BAR, along with the planet's name, is the date—the elapsed time since the planet was created. In the SPEED MENU you can change the format of the date between RELATIVE DATE (time elapsed since the beginning of the present Time Scale) and ABSOLUTE DATE (time elapsed since the creation of the planet). Since this planet is in the first Time Scale, the two are the same.

There will be no oceans for a while, and there is no atmosphere to burn up incoming meteors.

Sit back for a couple minutes and watch, switching between the EDIT and MAP WINDOWS. You will witness events: meteor strikes, volcanos, and earthquakes. Soon oceans will form and life will form in the oceans.

TOURING THE PLANET

Bring the EDIT WINDOW to the front, and make it as big as you can. Scroll around the planet and go sightseeing for a few minutes.

A lot is going on: time is passing very fast in this Time Scale. You can see the continents drifting. Single-celled life is spreading. Meteors hit the land and make craters that become lakes or hit the ocean and cause tidal waves.

EDIT WINDOW CONTROL PANEL

Bring the EDIT WINDOW to the front and look at the EDIT WINDOW CONTROL PANEL. At the top-left of the panel are six icons. Click on these icons to activate tools for changing the planet. Below that is the CURRENT TOOL DISPLAY. It shows which tool is being used and the cost in energy to use it.

Click on each icon. The three on the left have submenus. Click and hold to see them. Keep the mouse button down, and slide the pointer to an option on the submenu to select it.

To get an explanation of what an icon does, hold down the SHIFT KEY and click on the icon. The HELP WINDOW will explain what it does and how to use it.

Below the icons are the DATA LAYER BUTTONS—five buttons that let you decide what information about the planet will be displayed. You can have any, all, or none of these on at once.

You can also get HELP WINDOW messages about these buttons.

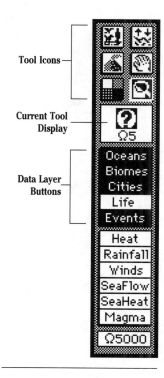

Tool Icons

Current Tool Display

Data Layer Buttons

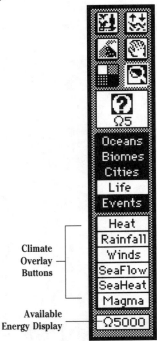

Oceans
Biomes
Cities
Life
Events

Heat
Rainfall
Winds
SeaFlow
SeaHeat
Magma

Ω5000

Climate Overlay Buttons

Available Energy Display

Click on these, and play with them. When you turn off the display of the oceans, you can see the elevation of the ocean floor. This doesn't make the ocean go away, it just makes it invisible. Depending on how fast you read, and how fast your computer is, you may or may not have life or biomes to turn on and off at this time.

Below the DATA LAYER BUTTONS are the CLIMATE OVERLAY BUTTONS—six buttons that let you turn on and off display of climactic information. Only one of these can be on at a time.

You can also get HELP WINDOW messages about these buttons.

Go ahead and play with these for a while.

At the bottom of the EDIT WINDOW CONTROL PANEL is the AVAILABLE ENERGY DISPLAY. In SimEarth, the price you pay to manipulate the planet is in energy. This little box tells you how much you have left. As time passes, your energy supply will slowly build back up, but it will never exceed 5000 in an easy game, or 2000 in an average or hard game. In experimental mode, you have unlimited energy.

USING THE SET ALTITUDE TOOL

This tool has two modes: RAISE and LOWER. Click once on the SET ALTITUDE icon. The icon will be highlighted. In the CURRENT TOOL DISPLAY, you will see the SET ALTITUDE icon, but with only an up arrow along with the cost to use it: 50 Ω (energy units).

Only the up arrow is shown to indicate that this tool is in RAISE mode.

Ω50

Scroll the EDIT WINDOW to a place on the planet that is mostly water (make sure the display of oceans is on). Point to the water and click and hold for a few seconds. You've just built an island. If you watch for a while, you'll notice that the island moves and changes. That is because time is moving so fast in this Time Scale that you can see the continents moving (continental drift).

Now click on the SET ALTITUDE icon again. The icon in the CURRENT TOOL DISPLAY shows only a down arrow to indicate that the tool is in LOWER mode. The price to lower altitude is also 50 energy units.

Scroll over to a landmass, click and hold for a few seconds. You've just dug a lake.

THE GAIA WINDOW

Select GAIA from the WINDOWS MENU. A small window appears with a representation of Gaia—the planetary organism. This face will give you constant feedback on the "mood of the planet."

Gaia's mood is based on how well life on the planet is doing. The moods range from bliss to horror. Everything that happens and everything you do affects the planet's mood.

You may want to keep this window showing in a corner of the screen to give you constant feedback on your planetary management.

Gaia will sleep until life forms, then it will wake up. Its eyes will follow the pointer around the screen. Please don't poke it in the eye.

TRIGGERING EVENTS

Now for some real fun—triggering events. Make sure the EVENTS DATA LAYER BUTTON in the EDIT WINDOW CONTROL PANEL is on.

Events are more than just disasters or occurrences: they are tools. They can be helpful in shaping the land and changing the composition of the atmosphere. They can also cause mass extinctions.

Remember, in SimEarth, everything is interrelated. To see how each event can be used for good or bad, and its side effects that affect the planet, see the "Events" chapter of the Reference section and use the HELP function (hold the SHIFT KEY and click on the TRIGGER EVENTS icon).

METEORS

 Click and hold on the TRIGGER EVENT icon. You will see the submenu of events. Slide the pointer until METEOR is highlighted, then release the mouse button.

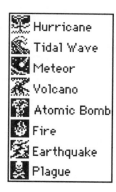

Scroll the EDIT WINDOW so water is showing. Click a few times on the ocean. Meteors will crash into the water, creating tidal waves. When meteors hit the water, they add a lot of moisture to the air, which will increase rainfall and contribute to the greenhouse effect. To check this, select AIR SAMPLE from the GRAPHS MENU, which will open the ATMOSPHERIC COMPOSITION GRAPH. Look at the percentage of Water Vapor. Go back to the EDIT WINDOW and drop a few more meteors in the ocean. Check the Water Vapor percentage again.

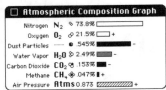

Atmospheric Composition Graph		
Nitrogen N_2	73.8%	
Oxygen O_2	21.5%	+
Dust Particles	.545%	−
Water Vapor H_2O	2.49%	−
Carbon Dioxide CO_2	.153%	−
Methane CH_4	.047%	+
Air Pressure Atms	0.873	+

Crash a few meteors into land. You will get huge craters. If they are deep enough, they will become lakes. Crashing meteors into land spews dust into the atmosphere. Too much dust in the air blocks sunlight, which will kill plants (biomes), which will kill animals. Check the dust levels in the ATMOSPHERIC COMPOSITION GRAPH before and after triggering meteors.

VOLCANOS
Click and hold on the TRIGGER EVENT icon again, and select VOLCANO from the submenu.

Trigger a volcano somewhere in the ocean—instant island. Volcanos in the water cause tidal waves, which can kill land life near the coasts. Volcanos also add dust and carbon dioxide to the atmosphere.

EARTHQUAKES
Now activate EARTHQUAKE on the TRIGGER EVENTS submenu. It has a sub-submenu for choosing the direction of the earthquake's energy. Earthquakes in SimEarth let you change the direction of the magma flow under the surface of the earth, which affects continental drift. In other words, earthquakes let you move continents. To easily see the results of earthquakes, turn on the MAGMA CLIMATE LAYER BUTTON.

Hurricane
Tidal Wave
Meteor
Volcano
Atomic Bomb
Fire
Earthquake
Plague

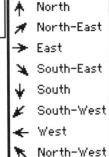

North
North-East
East
South-East
South
South-West
West
North-West

You can use earthquakes to build mountain ranges. Center the EDIT WINDOW over a landmass, preferably an area at a low altitude (you can use the SET ALTITUDE tool to lower it). Near the top of the window, set off a few earthquakes that expend their energy to the south. Near the bottom of the window, set off a few earthquakes that expend their energy to the north. This has the effect of squeezing the land from both sides, and a mountain range will be pushed up where the energy from the southbound and northbound quakes meet.

OTHER EVENTS
The other events work the same way—they are useful tools with both good and bad side effects. Take some time and play with them.

REPORT WINDOW

Open the WINDOWS MENU and select REPORT. The REPORT WINDOW tells you how you, your planet, and your planet's life are doing.

The information displayed in the REPORT WINDOW varies for each Time Scale. There is also a special REPORT WINDOW for the Daisyworld scenario and for the two terraforming scenarios (Mars and Venus).

At the bottom of the window is your CURRENT TASK. This is what must be accomplished before advancing to the next Time Scale, or successfully completing a scenario.

Let's start a new planet in the Civilization Time Scale and look at the rest of our tools.

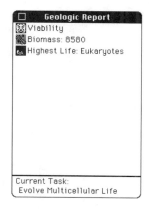

First, save the old planet to disk. Select SAVE AS... from the FILE MENU. Choose the disk or directory you want to save to, and change the name of the planet if you wish. Click the SAVE button. Refer to the SimEarth addendum for details.

Select NEW PLANET from the FILE MENU. This time, choose experimental mode, then click on the random planet.

When the Name and Time Scale dialog box appears, click in the box to the left of "Civilized," type in the name CIVWORLD, and click the BEGIN button.

CREATING A PLANET IN THE CIVILIZATION TIME SCALE

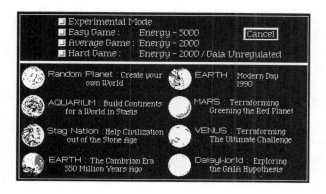

INVESTIGATING THE NEW WORLD
MAP WINDOW

Lets take a look around the new planet. Open the MAP WINDOW, if it isn't already open, and have it display the world in the flat projection (not the globe). At the bottom of the window is the MAP WINDOW CONTROL PANEL.

In this control panel are 12 icons that change the map display. They are arranged in five groups: Geosphere, Hydrosphere, Atmosphere, Bio(sphere), and Civ(ilization).

The map now displayed is the Terrain Map, which corresponds with the Terrain Map icon. Here you can see the continents and the oceans, and the terrain level of the land. Click on the INFO BUTTON in the lower-right corner of the window. The INFO BOX now displays a legend to the map's altitude.

Click on the Event Map icon. Now the map shows the land and water (no altitude), plus tiny symbols that appear where events are occurring (if they are occurring). The INFO BOX shows a legend to the event symbols.

Click on the Drift Map icon. Now you see the direction of the magma currents, which controls continental drift on your planet.

Click on the Terrain Map icon. The drift is gone, and the altitude display is back.

The first icon in the Hydrosphere group is the Hide/Show Oceans icon. This toggles on and off the view of the oceans. It can be used along with any of the other icons. Click on it a couple times, but when you are done, leave the display of oceans on.

Click on the Ocean Temperature icon. You are shown the temperature of the ocean in shades or colors. The INFO BOX displays a legend of the temperatures.

Click on the next icon to see a display of ocean currents.

Now for the Atmosphere group. The three icons in this group display Air Temperature, Rainfall, and Air Currents, respectively. Click on each of them. The INFO BOX will display a legend for each display.

The Biosphere group only has two icons: Biomes shows the biome distribution on the planet, and Life shows the diversity of life on the planet. Once again, the INFO BOX displays a legend to help you interpret the map.

There is only one icon in the Civilization group. It displays the distribution of the seven levels of Technology on the planet.

GRAPHS

The graphs will also give you information about this planet. Select BIOMES from the GRAPHS MENU to see the BIOME RATIO GRAPH.

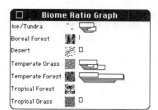

This graph shows the relative amounts of each biome on the planet. Since it shows changes over time, you can see the rise and fall of biomes through time.

Select LIFE-FORMS from the GRAPHS MENU to see the LIFE CLASS RATIO GRAPH. This shows the relative amounts of each class of life on the planet.

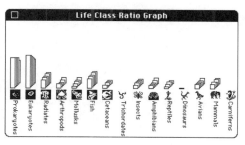

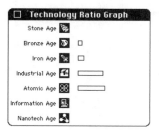

Select TECHNOLOGY from the GRAPHS MENU to see the TECHNOLOGY RATIO GRAPH. This shows the relative amount of each level of technology on the planet.

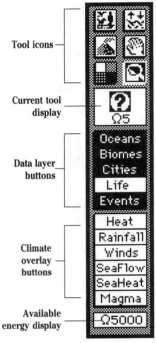

Tool icons

Current tool display

Data layer buttons

Climate overlay buttons

Available energy display

EDIT WINDOW

Go back to the EDIT WINDOW, and look at the EDIT WINDOW CONTROL PANEL. Turn on all the DATA LAYER BUTTONS.

 Click on the EXAMINE icon. Now click and hold on any spot in the EDIT WINDOW DISPLAY AREA. A small window will pop up on the screen that gives you data on the biomes, life, and civilization in that spot.

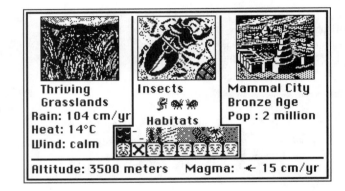

While still holding down the mouse button, move the pointer around the EDIT WINDOW. The data window will update to describe the spot under the pointer. Take some time and use the EXAMINE tool to explore your world.

If you ask for HELP (hold down the SHIFT KEY and click) in the EDIT WINDOW DISPLAY AREA it will bring up the same data window as the EXAMINE tool.

Now that we know something about the planet, let's shake things up a little.

THE PLACE LIFE TOOL

Make sure the EDIT WINDOW is displayed, and the LIFE and CITIES DATA LAYER BUTTONS are on. Click and hold on the PLACE LIFE icon.

You will see a submenu. This is where you choose life, civilizations (cities), and terraformers to place on your planet.

The left side of the submenu is for selecting life. The top seven are sea life, the bottom seven are land life.

On the right side, the top seven items are cities for your intelligent SimEarthlings. The seven cities represent seven levels of technology. Below the cities are seven terraformers. These are tools that you will need to terraform Mars and Venus.

Select one of the life-forms on the left side of the submenu. Move the pointer to the EDIT WINDOW DISPLAY AREA and click. The life-form will be placed where you click.

Depending on the Time Scale and level of development on the planet, some of the options on the Place Life submenu will not be available. These include both life-forms and cities.

Prokaryote	Stone Age
Eukaryote	Bronze Age
Radiate	Iron Age
Arthropod	Industrial Age
Mollusk	Atomic Age
Fish	Info Age
Cetacean	Nanotech Age
Trichordate	Biome Factory
Insect	Oxygenator
Amphibian	N2 Generator
Reptile	Hydrator
Dinosaur	CO2 Generator
Avian	Monolith
Mammal	Ice Meteor

Just because you place life on the planet doesn't mean it will stay there. If you place ocean life on the land or land life in the water, it won't last long. Also, life-forms can only survive well in certain biomes.

A complete chart of what life can live in which biome is in the "Life" chapter in the Reference section of this manual.

Notice that placing different life-forms and cities costs different amounts of energy, depending on the level of advancement of the item you are placing.

THE PLANT BIOME TOOL

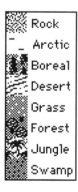

Just as you can place animal life on the planet, you can plant biomes. Click and hold on the PLANT BIOME icon. You will see a submenu that will allow you to choose a biome to plant.

Rock
Arctic
Boreal
Desert
Grass
Forest
Jungle
Swamp

The various biomes can only survive in certain climates—if you plant a swamp in a polar icecap, it won't last long. A complete chart of what biomes can survive in which climates is in the "Life" chapter in the Reference section.

When planting biomes, you can click and hold the mouse button, and slowly drag the mouse across the planet. The biomes will be continuously "painted" onto the terrain.

THE MOVE TOOL

 The last tool in the EDIT WINDOW is for moving biomes, life, and cities. Click on the MOVE icon.

Move the pointer to the EDIT WINDOW DISPLAY AREA and click and hold on a spot with life, a city, or a biome. Move the pointer to a different spot, and release the mouse button.

Besides moving things, the MOVE tool is helpful for investigation. When you have multiple data layers on, LIFE symbols will cover BIOME symbols, and CITY symbols will cover both LIFE and BIOMES. To see what life or biome is under a city, use the MOVE tool to lift it, then put it back in the same place.

We've covered exploration and modification of the planet; now we'll learn how to modify the simulation.

MODIFYING THE SIMULATION

INTRODUCTION

In the EDIT WINDOW you change the planet. In fact, you only change part of the planet. With the MODEL CONTROL PANELS, you make changes to the actual model that controls the fate of the entire planet.

There are four MODEL CONTROL PANELS. One each to modify the simulation in the following areas:

> GEOSPHERE—the planet itself;
> ATMOSPHERE—the planet's air and climate;
> BIOSPHERE—life on the planet; and
> CIVILIZATION—the behavior of the planet's sentient species.

This tutorial won't explain each and every control on each CONTROL PANEL. It will explain what each CONTROL PANEL does, and how to use it. For a complete description of the control panels, see the "Model Control Panels" chapter in the Reference section.

You can also find out what each control does by using the HELP function: hold down the SHIFT KEY and click on one of the controls. A HELP WINDOW will appear with a description of what each individual control does.

GEOSPHERE MODEL CONTROL PANEL

The GEOSPHERE MODEL CONTROL PANEL controls the geologic aspects of a planet. These aspects, such as continental drift and core formation, change very slowly over millions of years. Since they change so slowly, the only way to see them clearly is in the Geologic Time Scale.

Create a new, random planet in the Geologic Time Scale.

Close all the windows, except the MAP WINDOW. Open the GEOSPHERE MODEL CONTROL PANEL. You can either do this by selecting GEOSPHERE from the MODELS MENU, or by clicking on the GEOSPHERE button in the MAP WINDOW CONTROL PANEL.

Open the OPTIONS MENU and make sure UPDATE BACKGROUND is on. (It will have a checkmark on the left if it is on.) This will allow you to keep the MODEL CONTROL PANEL in front, and still see the changes in the MAP WINDOW.

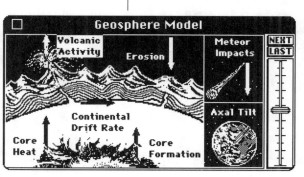

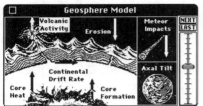

There are seven controls on this panel. Each control has a name and an indicator. The indicator is usually an arrow. For this tutorial, we'll concentrate on the CONTINENTAL DRIFT control because the results of changing it are easy to see.

Click on the words CONTINENTAL DRIFT in the GEOSPHERE MODEL CONTROL PANEL. The words and the arrow above those words will be highlighted to show that this control is ready for your changes.

To change the settings, you will use the slider control on the right side of the control panel. Click above or below the slider to move it up or down one notch. You can also click and drag the slider.

If the oceans haven't formed yet on your newest planet, wait a minute until they do, then continue.

Click and drag the slider all the way to the top, turning continental drift to its maximum setting. Go to the SPEED MENU and set the simulator to FAST. Watch the MAP WINDOW for a while: you will actually see the continents moving.

Now turn the continental drift all the way down. The continents will slow their movement to nearly nothing.

The other controls are operated the same way, and though the results of changing them isn't as obvious as with continental drift, they all have a powerful impact on the planet.

ATMOSPHERE MODEL CONTROL PANEL

Now open the ATMOSPHERE MODEL CONTROL PANEL. You can open it three ways: select ATMOSPHERE from the MODELS MENU, click on the ATMOSPHERE button on the MAP WINDOW CONTROL PANEL, or click the NEXT button in the upper-right corner of the GEOSPHERE MODEL CONTROL PANEL.

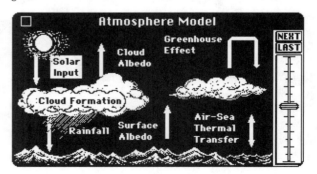

The ATMOSPHERE MODEL CONTROL PANEL is effective in all four Time Scales.

 Bring the MAP WINDOW to the front, and click on the AIR TEMPERA-TURE icon. Click on the INFO BUTTON to display a color/shade legend of the temperatures.

Bring the ATMOSPHERE MODEL CONTROL PANEL to the front. Click on SOLAR INPUT, then drag the slider all the way to the top. You just turned the heat from the Sun to maximum. Your planet will soon start warming up.

To add insult to injury, turn GREENHOUSE EFFECT all the way up, and turn CLOUD ALBEDO, SURFACE ALBEDO, and AIR-SEA THERMAL TRANSFER all the way down. Each of these actions will contribute to global warming.

Click on the INFO BUTTON. It will now display a graph of the changes in air temperature. Watch for a while. Soon the map and graph will show a rise in temperature. If you leave it rising long enough, your oceans will boil off and all life on the planet will die.

After a few minutes, set all the settings back to midway, and watch the map and graph as everything begins to cool down.

BIOSPHERE MODEL CONTROL PANEL

The BIOSPHERE MODEL CONTROL PANEL is most effective in Evolution Time Scale, but has some effect in the other Time Scales. It controls how the simulation models life on the planet.

Create a new planet in the Evolution Time Scale, set the simulation speed to FAST in the SPEED MENU, and open the BIOSPHERE MODEL CONTROL PANEL. It can be opened from the menu, the MAP WINDOW CONTROL PANEL, or the NEXT button on the ATMOSPHERE MODEL CONTROL PANEL.

Turn ADVANCE RATE, MUTATION RATE, and REPRODUCTION RATE on the BIOSPHERE MODEL CONTROL PANEL all the way up.

The changes from this control panel are much less obvious than the others. You can best see them in the HISTORY WINDOW.

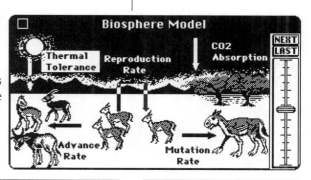

| HISTORY WINDOW

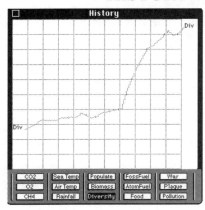

Open the HISTORY WINDOW by selecting HISTORY in the WINDOWS MENU.

The HISTORY WINDOW displays the changes in 15 factors over time. Click on the DIVERSITY button to display the changing number of species on the planet.

Watch for a few minutes, and the changes you made in the BIOSPHERE MODEL CONTROL PANEL will cause a rise in the diversity.

CIVILIZATION MODEL CONTROL PANEL

The CIVILIZATION MODEL CONTROL PANEL controls how the model deals with your intelligent species. It is only useful in the Civilization and Technology Time Scales.

Open the CIVILIZATION MODEL CONTROL PANEL. This control panel is one of the main challenges of SimEarth. You decide what energy sources the intelligent inhabitants of your planet will invest their time in, and what they will do with the energy.

This is a very complex control panel. For a complete explanation, see the "MODEL CONTROL PANEL" chapter in the Reference section of this manual.

The left side of the CIVILIZATION MODEL CONTROL PANEL is for choosing the energy sources to develop. These are set the same as settings on the other control panels. Different energy sources are appropriate for different levels of technology: you can make a Stone Age level civilization spend a lot of time trying to develop nuclear energy, but they don't have the knowledge or tools to succeed, and won't get any return from it.

The more you invest in energy forms that are appropriate for the technology level, the more energy the civilizations will have to use for advancement to the next technology level.

The right side of the control panel is where you allocate energy. You decide to what use the civilizations will put the energy they produce.

This side of the control panel works a little differently from the left side. It is a ratio. All energy that is produced is used. The higher the setting for each energy use, the higher the percentage of the produced energy will be allocated to that use. If the settings are all in the middle, or all the way up, the model interprets it the same. The important thing here is the relative settings of each energy use. Set your priorities and allocate to those uses you find most important.

The CIVILIZATION MODEL CONTROL PANEL is closely related to the REPORT WINDOW.

REPORT WINDOW

Create a new planet in the Technology Time Scale. Make sure the UPDATE BACKGROUND option is on.

Open the REPORT WINDOW, and arrange the screen so it and the CIVILIZATION MODEL CONTROL PANEL are both visible.

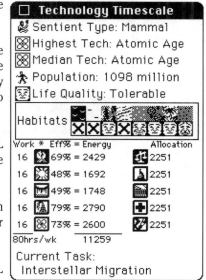

Take a look at the REPORT WINDOW. There is detailed information on the planet's civilized life. It tells you the class of your sentient species, the highest and average (median) technology level, the population, and quality of life. It also shows a chart of what biomes your sentient species prefers to live in.

Below that is a section on energy that relates to the CIVILIZATION MODEL CONTROL PANEL. It lists the energy sources, and their efficiency. The efficiency depends on the average level of technology on your planet.

To the left of each energy source are the hours per week your global citizen works on this energy source. Below these hours are the total hours per week intelligent SimEarthlings must work to survive.

As you turn the energy investments on the CIVILIZATION MODEL CONTROL PANEL up and down, the hours worked will rise and fall. Try it.

Keep this in mind when you set your energy investment—the work hours per week affect the SimEarthling's quality of life.

ALLOCATING ENERGY

Energy allocation in the CIVILIZATION MODEL CONTROL PANEL affects every aspect of the sentient SimEarthling's lives.

The results of your allocation are easy to see. Make sure the UPDATE BACKGROUND option is on.

For an easy-to-see example, we'll look at PHILOSOPHY.

Allocating to PHILOSOPHY lessens the frequency and severity of war. If you take all allocation away from PHILOSOPHY, wars will break out all over the planet. These wars can be viewed in the EDIT WINDOW and the HISTORY WINDOW.

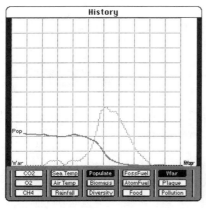

Open the HISTORY WINDOW and arrange the screen so you can see it along with the CIVILIZATION MODEL CONTROL PANEL. In the HISTORY WINDOW, turn the POPULATE and WAR graphs on. Turn PHILOSOPHY all the way down in the CIVILIZATION MODEL CONTROL PANEL.

The occurrence of war will quickly rise. Eventually it will fall, because so many of the sentient SimEarthlings have been killed that there's no one left to fight.

Allocating or not allocating to the other energy uses can have results as drastic as PHILOSOPHY. These results can be seen in the EDIT, REPORT and MAP WINDOWS. Try turning each one all the way up, then all the way down and see what happens.

Allocating to SCIENCE will help your intelligent SimEarthlings advance to higher levels of technology. No allocation to SCIENCE will cause advancement to stop. Allocate too much and they will advance too fast, and kill themselves.

Allocating to AGRICULTURE affects the food supply.

Allocating to MEDICINE affects the frequency and severity of plagues.

Allocating to ART/MEDIA affects the quality of life on your planet.

Your task here is making difficult choices and setting priorities.

CONCLUSION

Now you know the basics of SimEarth:

Using menus;
Opening and closing windows;
Creating and saving planets;
Getting information from maps and graphs;
Changing the planet in the EDIT WINDOW; and
Changing the simulation in the MODEL CONTROL PANELS.

Mastery of planet management takes a lot of time and experimentation. You may even (heaven forbid) have to read the rest of this manual.

Happy simulating.

UNBLANK PAGE

To keep this manual consistent by always having a chapter title page on the right side, we either had to leave this page blank, say something dumb like "This page intentionally left blank," or fill it up with something.

Here are some profound thoughts and revelations that occurred to us while playing SimEarth.

EVOLUTIONARY THOUGHT

In general, SimEarthlings are as lazy as Earthlings. They never want to work, and especially hate physical labor. Whenever there are heavy objects to move, they argue over who has to do it.

"I don't want to carry it—you carry it!"
"Not me—you carry it."

And that's how *Eu*karyotes evolved.

Of course, the usual solution is to hire a professional to do the work. That's what *Pro*karyotes do for a living.

REVELATION #1

When you're sitting on top of the world, be careful not to break the monitor.

SIMEARTHLING EXTINCT BLUES

My life-form's gone, but I don't worry,
'Cause I'm simulating on top of the world.

NOBODY READS GAME MANUALS

Hi Mom. I know nobody reads game manuals, but I knew *you* would. I worked real hard on this manual, and...Mom...wake up Mom.

QUESTION

Where in the world *is* Carmen SimDiego?

REFERENCE

SimEarth

SimEarth

CONTROLLING THE SIMULATION

OF MICE AND KEYBOARDS

Depending on your computer, you may or may not have a mouse. If you do have one, then you will want to use it—SimEarth is much easier to control with a mouse than with a keyboard.

See the addendum for your computer for more information on using mice and keyboards in SimEarth.

In general, you will use the mouse to select items from menus, and to activate tools by clicking on icons. Once tools are activated, SimEarth functions much like a paint program that "paints life on a planet."

INPUT AND OUTPUT

SimEarth has a lot of windows, graphs, and control panels, and can get confusing. The easiest way to understand the program is to know where you can INPUT information—add or change the planet or model to suit yourself—and where to see OUTPUT, the information about the planet and results of your INPUT.

INPUT

There are three places to INPUT information: the FILE MENU, the EDIT WINDOW, and the MODEL CONTROL PANELS.

FILE MENU

By selecting NEW PLANET or LOAD PLANET from the FILE MENU, you remove the existing planet or scenario from memory and load another planet or scenario into the simulation.

EDIT WINDOW

The EDIT WINDOW is where you place life, change altitudes and trigger events. When you do these things, you are INPUTTING DATA—changes to the planet. Since this only affects the planet in the locale of your input, we call this LOCAL INPUT.

The EDIT WINDOW is also a source of OUTPUT.

MODEL CONTROL PANELS
The four MODEL CONTROL PANELS are where you change the actual model. These changes affect the entire planet, and change the simulation itself. Since everything—the whole world—is affected, we call this GLOBAL INPUT.

The MODEL CONTROL PANELS are the only places in SimEarth that are INPUT ONLY.

OUTPUT
Other than the MODEL CONTROL PANELS, every window in SimEarth gives OUTPUT—information for you about the planet, the simulation, and the results of your input.

MENUS

FILE MENU

The FILE MENU is for performing file and disk-related functions.

NEW PLANET brings up the NEW PLANET WINDOW, which allows you to pick any of the seven included Scenarios, or a new, randomly generated planet/game in any of three difficulty levels or experimental mode.

First, choose the difficulty level. There are three levels of difficulty for games: easy, medium, and hard. There is also an experimental mode that gives you an unlimited energy budget for planet manipulation.

Next, pick a scenario or a random planet. If you choose random planet, you will be shown a dialog box allowing you to name your new world, choose the Time Scale, and either begin the new planet or cancel. If you have a planet in progress that has not been saved, you will be given the opportunity to save it before the new planet is generated.

LOAD PLANET brings up a dialog box to allow you to load in a pre-existing planet. If you have a planet in progress that has not been saved, you will be given the opportunity to save it before loading a new one. See the SimEarth addendum for your computer for details on loading planets.

SAVE PLANET saves your current planet to disk. If it has not been saved before, it will bring up a dialog box window to allow you to name your planet before saving it. See the SimEarth addendum for your computer for details on saving planets.

SAVE AS brings up a dialog box, allowing you to change the name and/or location of a previously saved planet.

PRINT or **SNAPSHOT** may or may not be present in your version of SimEarth. See the SimEarth addendum for your machine for details.

QUIT ends your SimEarth session, with a final chance to save your planet-in-progress.

WINDOWS MENU

The WINDOWS MENU allows access to the various windows in SimEarth.

EDIT opens and/or brings the EDIT WINDOW to the front.

MAP opens and/or brings the MAP WINDOW to the front.

GAIA opens the GAIA WINDOW, which displays the face of the planet and gives constant feedback on your actions and the state of life in the world.

HISTORY opens and/or brings the HISTORY WINDOW to the front.

REPORT opens and/or brings the REPORT WINDOW to the front.

TUTORIAL opens and/or brings the TUTORIAL WINDOW to the front.

GLOSSARY opens a HELP WINDOW that displays a glossary of many earth science terms used in SimEarth.

MODELS MENU

The MODELS MENU allows access to the various MODEL CONTROL PANELS that let you adjust the inner workings of the simulation.

GEOSPHERE opens the Geosphere Model Control Panel.

ATMOSPHERE opens the Atmosphere Model Control Panel.

BIOSPHERE opens the Biosphere Model Control Panel.

CIVILIZATION opens the Civilization Model Control Panel.

GRAPHS MENU

The GRAPHS MENU allows access to the various graphs used in SimEarth.

AIR SAMPLE brings up the Atmospheric Composition graph.

BIOMES brings up the Biome Ratio graph.

LIFE-FORMS brings up the Life Class Ratio graph.

TECHNOLOGY brings up the Technology Ratio graph.

OPTIONS MENU

The OPTIONS MENU lets you adjust many features of SimEarth to suit your personal preferences. When the options are active, a checkmark will appear to the left of the option.

GOTO EVENTS automatically transports you to the location of any event that occurs. When this option is active, and when the EDIT WINDOW is in the front,

---

the area viewed in the EDIT WINDOW will jump to center on any events that occur. The default setting is off.

UPDATE BACKGROUND lets you choose whether or not all windows on the screen will be animated and constantly updated. When this option is inactive, only the front window will be animated and updated. Having this option on greatly decreases the speed of the simulation. The default setting depends on your machine's speed of operation.

This is especially useful for high-speed machines with large monitors. If SimEarth runs too slowly, or you rarely display more than one or two windows at a time, you may wish to turn this off.

COMPRESS EDIT SCREEN is an option that can be very useful on computers with small screens. When active, it changes the EDIT WINDOW so it only displays every other tile, allowing you to see four times as much area. The default setting is off.

Normal view	Compressed view

MUSIC enables and disables music during the game. The default setting is on.

SOUND EFFECTS enables and disables sound during the game. The default setting is on.

MESSAGES enables and disables the display of messages to you from the simulator and the SimEarthlings that will appear throughout the game. The default setting is on.

AUTOSCROLL allows automatic scrolling of the terrain in the EDIT WINDOW when using any of the EDIT WINDOW icons near or at the edge of the window. The default setting is on.

SAVE OPTIONS + WINDOWS saves your present configuration of options, open windows, window sizes and window locations to disk as the default configuration. You can use this option again at any time to change the default settings.

SPEED MENU

The SPEED MENU allows you to set the simulation speed and date options.

FAST sets the simulation speed to the maximum available for your machine.

MODERATE sets the simulation speed to approximately 75% of the fast setting. This is the default speed setting.

SLOW sets the simulation speed to approximately 25% of the fast setting.

PAUSE pauses the simulation. All the planet manipulation tools will be available and active, but time will be stopped.

RELATIVE DATE displays the date as the number of years since the beginning of the present Time Scale. This is the default date setting.

ABSOLUTE DATE displays the date as the number of years since the original cooling of the planet. If you began your planet in a later Time Scale, Absolute Date will estimate and add the time from earlier Time Scales.

DATASOUND MENU

The DATASOUND MENU controls the sound functions in SimEarth. The first two items are ways of using the sound, and the last seven items let you choose the data from which the sound will be generated.

TONE MONITOR plays an intermittent, recurrent tone based on one of the data settings. This is used for aural monitoring of data. For instance, if you are trying to combat global warming, you could set the tone monitor to report on air temperature. Every so often you will hear a tone. The higher the tone, the higher the average global temperature. You will hear the changes in temperature without having to look at the air temperature map.

PLAY DATA SONG is an option that is more fun than useful. It takes 32 evenly spaced samples of the selected data from the top to the bottom of the map, averages the values across the map, and plays them as notes. For example, if air temperature is selected, then the data song will convert the 32 data samples into 32 notes—the higher the air temperature, the higher the pitch. The notes will be lowest around the poles and highest near the equator.

ALTITUDE bases the sound on data in the Altitude array.

AIR TEMPERATURE bases the sound on data in the Air Temperature array.

RAINFALL bases the sound on data in the Rainfall array.

SEA TEMPERATURE bases the sound on data in the Sea Temperature array.

BIOMASS bases the sound on data in the Biome array.

LIFE bases the sound on data in the Life array.

CIVILIZATION bases the sound on data in the Humans array.

There are many different windows in SimEarth. Here is a complete description of each one.

WINDOWS

There is on-screen help available for almost everything in SimEarth, including all menus, buttons, icons, tools, graphs, and control panels.

HELP WINDOW

Help windows are not available through the menus. To get HELP, press and hold the SHIFT KEY. This will change your cursor to HELP MODE. Then click on any item on the screen, and you will be shown a text window with lots of information about that item.

HELP

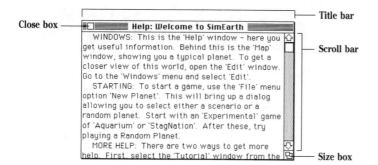

Close box ——— Title bar

Scroll bar

Size box

If you ask for HELP in the DISPLAY AREA of the EDIT WINDOW, you will get the same information window that is produced by the EXAMINE icon.

If you ask for HELP in the DISPLAY AREA of the MAP WINDOW, you will get information on the active MAP WINDOW display.

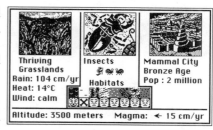

There is a massive amount of information available in the HELP WINDOW. Almost anything in the world (simulated, that is) that you want to know about is in there.

The HELP WINDOW is your friend. Use it.

The on-line GLOSSARY is useful for getting help with definitions of words in the program you may not be familiar with. The GLOSSARY is available in the WINDOWS MENU.

This is really a dialog box, not a window, but it is so important that for the purposes of this manual, we are giving it a promotion.

Use this window for creating new, random planets, and for starting the scenarios.

At the top of the window are settings that let you choose the difficulty of the game or scenario. At the bottom of the window are the scenarios and random planet buttons.

Any random planet or scenario can be played in Experimental Mode, Easy Game, Average Game, or Hard Game.

Help is available on every setting and button in this window. Hold down the SHIFT KEY and click on anything in the window to receive help. You can get explanations of all the options and scenarios before beginning a game.

SETTINGS
Use these settings to adjust difficulty levels for all games, scenarios, random planets, and experiments. Just click on the button next to a setting to choose it.

EXPERIMENTAL MODE allows you to load any of the scenarios or a random planet and have unlimited energy for planet manipulation. With the unlimited energy, you can set up any type of planet you want in any stage of development, and add any other factors or conditions you want. This mode is really a "planetary spreadsheet."

This is also a good mode for learning SimEarth.

The MODEL CONTROL PANELS will all be randomly set at "moderate" values that should allow planetary progress without many changes.

EASY GAME is good for beginners. In an easy game, life appears and evolves quickly and easily. In fact, it will take some effort on your part to stop it.

Your starting energy level is 5000 E.U. (energy units)

The MODEL CONTROL PANELS will all be randomly set at "moderate" values.

AVERAGE GAME is a little more challenging. It will take some effort on your part to get your planet progressing and keep it going.

Your starting energy level is 2000 E.U.

The MODEL CONTROL PANELS will all be randomly set at "extreme" values that will require some fine tuning.

HARD GAME is really difficult. In fact, it's really very difficult. Not only will you have to adjust the MODEL CONTROL PANELS, but you will have to take on the role of Gaia.

The MODEL CONTROL PANELS will all be randomly set at "extreme" values that will require some fine tuning.

All Gaian regulation of climate, atmosphere and life is turned off and there will be no spontaneous generation of life—it's all in your hands.

CANCEL removes the NEW PLANET WINDOW in case you change your mind.

PLANETS AND SCENARIOS

Any planet or scenario can be played in Easy, Medium, or Hard Game as well as Experimental Mode. For in-depth descriptions of the scenarios see the "Scenarios" chapter of this manual. Just click on one of the planets to choose it.

RANDOM PLANET creates a randomly generated planet in any of the four Time Scales. When you choose this option, you will be shown a dialog box that will let you pick the Time Scale and name the planet.

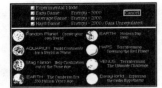

AQUARIUM is a planet with no continents. It is a good starting point for those who like to design their own landmasses. It is in the Evolution Time Scale.

STAG NATION is a planet in the early Civilization Time Scale. Sentient life on this planet is limited to one small island. You can help it spread, or eliminate it and try to bring another life-form to intelligence.

EARTH CAMBRIAN ERA is a simulation of Earth in the Evolution Time Scale. One of the best features of this scenario is that its continental drift recreates the real Earth's drift.

EARTH MODERN DAY gives you a chance to take over the Earth of today. You'll get to deal with all the problems we deal with in the real world. This scenario is not recommended for escapists.

MARS gives you the chance to terraform Mars and turn it into a planet capable of supporting Earth life-forms.

VENUS gives you the ultimate challenge in terraforming.

DAISYWORLD is the original, simpler version of the SimEarth simulation. Daisyworld was originally devised by James Lovelock as a demonstration of the Gaia theory.

The EDIT WINDOW is a close-up view of your planet. It is used for LOCAL INPUT—making changes to the planet, and for OUTPUT—investigating the planet and seeing the results of your input.

The EDIT WINDOW consists of four major parts: the TITLE BAR, the DISPLAY AREA, the SCROLL BARS, and the EDIT WINDOW CONTROL PANEL.

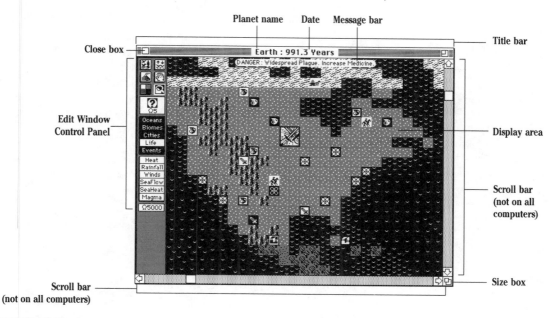

TITLE BAR

Located at the top of the EDIT WINDOW, the TITLE BAR displays the name of your planet and the date. The date can displayed as either the RELATIVE date or the ABSOLUTE date, selected from the SPEED MENU.

On the left side of the TITLE BAR is the CLOSE BOX. Clicking in this box will close the EDIT WINDOW. The window can be reopened by selecting the item "EDIT" from the WINDOWS MENU.

On the right side of the TITLE BAR is the GROW BOX. Clicking in this box will make the EDIT WINDOW grow until it fills the entire screen. Clicking it again will return the window to its former size.

The EDIT WINDOW can be moved around the screen by clicking and dragging the TITLE BAR.

EDIT WINDOW DISPLAY AREA

This is where you are shown your planet in a close-up view. The information you are shown here is controlled by the EDIT WINDOW CONTROL PANEL.

There are two scales that can be shown in this display: Normal and Compressed. If you select "Compress Edit Screen" from the OPTIONS MENU, this window will only display every other tile. This will give you less exact information, but will show you four times as much of the area of your planet as the Normal view. This is especially useful on machines with small screens (Mac Plus, SE, SE/30). This is the view that prints out with the PRINT option on the FILE MENU.

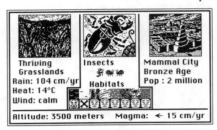

Using the HELP function (hold the SHIFT KEY and click) in the EDIT WINDOW DISPLAY AREA will bring up a window detailing all the information that the simulation has about the spot where you clicked.

Messages from the simulation and the SimEarthlings will sometimes appear at the top of the display area.

TERRAIN AND ELEVATION

There are 32 levels of terrain. The lighter the shade, the higher the altitude. Each different shade represents a change of 500 meters. Since altitude is measured from sea level, and sea level can be anywhere—or nowhere—there is no exact altitude that can be assigned to each shade.

There are three types of sea displays, depending on the depth of the water.

 SHELF—0 to 1000 meters deep

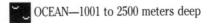 OCEAN—1001 to 2500 meters deep

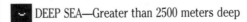 DEEP SEA—Greater than 2500 meters deep

SCROLLING THE TERRAIN

Depending on your computer, there may or may not be SCROLL BARS along the right and bottom of the EDIT WINDOW. If they are there, you can use them to scroll the terrain in the EDIT WINDOW to see different parts of the planet. Click on the arrows or the bars, or drag the scroll box to cause scrolling.

If there are no SCROLL BARS, then scrolling is accomplished by moving the pointer to any edge or corner of the screen. For keyboard-controlled scrolling, see the SimEarth addendum for your machine.

SIZE BOX

In the lower-right corner of the window is the SIZE BOX. Clicking and dragging this box will allow you to re-size the EDIT WINDOW.

EDIT WINDOW CONTROL PANEL

This control panel is for controlling both the information viewed in the EDIT WINDOW and for accessing the tools for planet modification.

Using the HELP function (hold the SHIFT KEY and click) in the CONTROL PANEL will bring up a small window with information about each of the items and buttons.

There are four sections to the EDIT WINDOW CONTROL PANEL: the TOOL ICONS, the CURRENT TOOL DISPLAY, the DATA LAYER BUTTONS, and the CLIMATE OVERLAY BUTTONS.

TOOL ICONS

By clicking on these icons, you access the tools for modifying your planet. There are six icons, three of which have submenus. Just below the Tool Icons is a box displaying the active icon and giving budget information for using that tool.

Every time you use one of the TOOL ICONS it will deplete your precious energy stores.

PLACE LIFE allows you to choose and place life and cities on the planet. This icon also allows you access to various terraforming tools for use on Mars and Venus.

Use this tool to spread life on the planet, to set various life-forms in competition with each other, and to test living conditions for various life-forms.

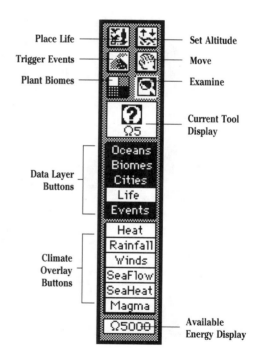

Prokaryote	Stone Age
Eukaryote	Bronze Age
Radiate	Iron Age
Arthropod	Industrial Age
Mollusk	Atomic Age
Fish	Info Age
Cetacean	Nanotech Age
Trichordate	Biome Factory
Insect	Oxygenator
Amphibian	N2 Generator
Reptile	Hydrator
Dinosaur	CO2 Generator
Avian	Monolith
Mammal	Ice Meteor

To select a life-form, city, or terraformer, click and hold on the PLACE LIFE icon. A submenu will appear. While holding the mouse button down, move the pointer to highlight the life, city, or terraformer of your choice, and then release the button.

Your choice will appear in the CURRENT TOOL DISPLAY, just below the icons, along with the cost in energy to place or use it.

To place the life, city, or terraformer on the planet, point to a spot in the display area and click.

There are 15 classes of life in SimEarth, seven in the sea, and eight on land. Each class of life is represented in SimEarth by 16 species.

Only 14 of the classes of life are available in the PLACE LIFE tool. CARNIFERNS—mobile, carnivorous plants that can develop intelligence—will sometimes evolve, but cannot be placed.

There are seven types of cities, each representing a level of civilization and technology. Most levels of technology are represented by cities with three population densities. Each of these levels also has a travelling population that represents sentients moving around, as well as trade and communication. The exception to this is the Nanotech Age, which is the highest level of technology in SimEarth. It has four levels of density, and no travelling population: we assume that they have matter transporters for instantaneous moving of people and products.

There are seven terraformers.

A complete description of the 15 classes of life in SimEarth is found later in this manual, in the chapter "Life." A complete description of the cities is covered in the chapter "Civilization." The terraformers will be covered in detail here.

The classes of life and cities available to place, with their cost in energy, are:

SEA LIFE CLASSES

PROKARYOTE—Single-celled life with no nucleus (bacteria). 35 E.U.

EUKARYOTE—Single-celled life with nucleus (amebas). 70 E.U.

RADIATE—Simple multi-celled life (starfish). 105 E.U.

ARTHROPOD—Crabs, lobsters, and crayfish. 140 E.U.

MOLLUSK—Snails, clams, oysters, scallops, octopi, and squid. 175 E.U.

FISH—Fish. 210 E.U.

CETACEAN—Whales and dolphins. 245 E.U.

LAND LIFE CLASSES

TRICHORDATE—Simple animal with a three-chord spine. 280 E.U.

INSECT—You know what these are. 315 E.U.

AMPHIBIAN—Frogs, newts, and toads. 350 E.U.

REPTILE—lizards, snakes, and turtles. 385 E.U.

DINOSAUR—Great big, huge reptiles. 420 E.U.

AVIAN—Birds. 455 E.U.

MAMMAL—Humans, apes, rodents, dogs, cats, etc. 490 E.U.

CITIES

The dates mentioned below are for reference to Earth only, and do not necessarily correspond with dates in SimEarth.

STONE AGE—Oldest Human culture; used stone tools. 500 E.U.

BRONZE AGE—Began circa 3500 B.C.; used bronze tools. 1000 E.U.

IRON AGE—Began circa 1000 B.C.; used iron tools. 1500 E.U.

▐🏭▌ INDUSTRIAL AGE—Began in late 18th century with the use of powered machinery. 2000 E.U.

▐▌ ATOMIC AGE—Began in the 1950s with the use of atomic power. 2500 E.U.

▐💻▌ INFORMATION AGE—Begins circa 2000 A.D.—information is the most important tool. 3000 E.U.

▐▌ NANOTECH AGE—Begins sometime in the future, characterized by science and technology beyond our imagination. 3500 E.U.

TERRAFORMERS

Terraformers are tools for turning Venus and Mars into earth-like planets. They aren't needed on Earth, or planets that are earth-like to begin with, but go ahead and try them to see what happens. Once placed, Terraformers keep working. Don't place too many—the only way to stop one is to hit it with a Meteor, Fire, or a Volcano.

▐🏭▌ BIOME FACTORY—When terraforming Mars or Venus, place the Biome Factory instead of individual biomes. The Biome Factory, once placed, looks at the terrain and climate and starts producing the appropriate biome type that can survive there. It will also detect changes in climate, and change the biomes it produces to a type that will survive the changes. Biome Factories cost 500 E.U.

▐▌ OXYGENATOR—The Oxygenator takes carbon dioxide (CO_2) out of the atmosphere and spits out free oxygen. Life requires a certain percentage of oxygen, between 15 to 25%, to survive. Too much oxygen on a planet will cause fires. Since it lessens the CO_2, a greenhouse gas, the Oxygenator will help cool a hot planet. An Oxygenator costs 500 E.U.

▐▌ N_2 GENERATOR—The N_2 (nitrogen) Generator is used to increase atmospheric pressure on a planet. The atmospheric density affects the planet's temperature—a denser atmosphere allows the planet to retain more heat. The thinner the atmosphere, the colder the planet. Also, having a denser atmosphere with lots of N_2 stabilizes the percentages of the other gases. An N_2 Generator costs 500 E.U.

VAPORATOR—The Vaporator spews water vapor into the atmosphere, raising the overall humidity of the planet and increasing rainfall. A Vaporator costs 500 E.U.

CO_2 GENERATOR—The CO_2 Generator produces CO_2, which is necessary for plants to live. A CO_2 Generator costs 500 E.U.

MONOLITH—The Monolith isn't a Terraformer, but we didn't have anywhere else to put it in the program. It is an Evolution Speed-up Device (our thanks to Arthur C. Clark).

To use it, select the Monolith, then immediately click on a life-form. There is a one-in-three chance of that life-form suddenly mutating to a higher level, which immediately moves you to the next Time Scale. It costs 2500 E.U. to use a Monolith—whether or not it works.

The Monolith can't be used on all life-forms—if you try to use the Monolith on a life-form that cannot mutate, the program will beep at you, but there will be no energy charge.

A disadvantage to using the Monolith is that you could jump ahead into the civilization Time Scale before enough fossil fuels have been generated, and civilization will collapse. Also, you need a wide population base to advance to the next technology level. Don't rush to a new Time Scale at the expense of your population.

If you successfully use the Monolith in the Technology Time Scale, it will bring about the Exodus event.

ICE METEOR—The Ice Meteor is a huge chunk of ice that you can crash into a dry planet to add water to the planetary system. An Ice Meteor costs 500 E.U.

THE EXTINCT FUNCTION

An added feature of the PLACE LIFE tool is the EXTINCT FUNCTION. If you want to remove a particular class of life from the planet, hold down either the OPTION KEY or CONTROL KEY (depending on your machine), then click on the PLACE LIFE icon and select a life-form from the PLACE LIFE submenu. All occurrences of the life-form you chose will disappear.

The EXTINCT FUNCTION only works on life-forms—not on cities. If you want to eliminate a life-form, you must do it before it reaches sentience and builds cities.

 EVENT TRIGGER

The EVENT TRIGGER lets you select and activate various events at various places on your planet.

The simulation will cause events to occur automatically, depending on many factors including the age of the planet, the climate, air and water temperatures, and sea level.

There are 11 possible events that occur in SimEarth. Three of them, exodus, war and pollution, will occur, but cannot be triggered by the user.

By triggering events yourself, you can learn the effects these events have on local populations as well as to the planet as a whole.

To activate events, click and hold on the EVENT TRIGGER icon. A submenu will appear, giving you a choice of eight events. While the mouse button is still down, slide the pointer to the right so it highlights the event you want to place, and release the button.

The selected event will appear in the CURRENT TOOL DISPLAY, just below the icons, along with the cost in energy to trigger it.

Next, move the pointer to the DISPLAY AREA, and click the mouse button to trigger an event on your planet. Click again in another place to cause the same event.

A complete description of all events and their causes and effects will be covered in the chapter "Events."

The available events in SimEarth, and their cost in energy, are:

HURRICANE—High winds and rain. 50 E.U.

TIDAL WAVE—A huge, destructive ocean wave. 50 E.U.

METEOR—A huge rock from space that crashes into your planet. 50 E.U.

VOLCANO—An explosive leak in the planet's surface that spews molten rock. 50 E.U.

ATOMIC TEST—An atomic explosion. 50 E.U.

 FIRE—Hot stuff. 50 E.U.

EARTHQUAKE—Shake, rattle and roll. 50 E.U. Clicking and holding on the Earthquake icon brings up a submenu that allows you to direct the Earthquake's energies.

PLAGUE—A deadly disease. 50 E.U.

↑	North
↗	North-East
→	East
↘	South-East
↓	South
↙	South-West
←	West
↖	North-West

PLANT BIOME—allows you to place or plant biomes onto your planet.

A biome is a major ecological community of plants and animals. Biomes will automatically be placed on the planet by the simulation. Their quantity and location is primarily controlled by altitude, temperature, and rainfall.

With this tool you can place any of the biomes anywhere on the planet at any time. Of course, they won't necessarily stay there. An Arctic biome will not last long in the hot equatorial zone, and a Jungle will not thrive at a planet's pole.

Place biomes to experiment, and to help shape or speed up development on your planet.

To use this tool, click and hold on the PLANT BIOME icon. A submenu will appear, giving you a choice of eight biomes. While the mouse button is still down, slide the pointer to the right so it highlights the biome you want to plant, and release the button. The selected biome will appear in the CURRENT TOOL DISPLAY, just below the icons, along with the cost in energy to place it. There is an energy cost of 50 E.U. for each biome planted.

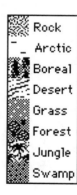

	Rock
	Arctic
	Boreal
	Desert
	Grass
	Forest
	Jungle
	Swamp

Next, move the pointer to the DISPLAY AREA, and click the mouse button to place a biome on your planet. The button can be held down while the mouse is slowly moved to place multiple segments. A click will be heard as each BIOME is placed. The pitch of the click will raise and lower with the terrain altitude.

A complete description of all the biomes in SimEarth will be found later in this manual in the chapter "Life." There are seven available biomes in SimEarth, plus ROCK, which represents a lack of a biome in a location.

BIOMES

ROCK—No biome.

ARCTIC—Can survive in a cold and dry climate.

BOREAL FOREST—Can survive in cold temperatures, with moderate to high rainfall.

DESERT—Can survive in moderate to hot temperatures, with very little rainfall.

TEMPERATE GRASSLANDS—Can survive in areas with moderate temperatures and rainfall.

FOREST—Can survive with moderate temperatures and high rainfall.

JUNGLE—Can survive with high temperatures and rainfall.

SWAMP—Can survive with high temperatures and moderate rainfall.

BIOME PREFERENCE CHART

	DRY (<30 cm/yr)	**MODERATE** (30–90 cm/yr)	**WET** (>90 cm/yr)
COLD (<0° C)	Arctic	Boreal Forest	Boreal Forest
MODERATE (0–25° C)	Desert	Temp. Grasslands	Forest
HOT (>25° C)	Desert	Swamp	Jungle

Biome preferences are also influenced by altitude and the amount of CO_2 in the atmosphere.

 SET ALTITUDE allows you to raise or lower sections of land. There are 32 possible levels of terrain in SimEarth.

Use this tool to raise or level mountain ranges, create islands in the ocean, or lakes in dry land. All these changes will have impact on climate, rainfall, local biomes, and local life-forms.

Click on the SET ALTITUDE icon. Look at the CURRENT TOOL DISPLAY. It shows that the SET ALTITUDE tool is active in "raise terrain" mode.

Move the pointer to the DISPLAY AREA. Click and hold the mouse button over land or water, and the land around the pointer will be raised in altitude, displayed by a lightening of the color or shade of the land.

Click on the SET ALTITUDE icon again, and look at the CURRENT TOOL DISPLAY. It shows that the SET ALTITUDE tool is active in "lower terrain" mode.

Move the pointer to the DISPLAY AREA. Click and hold the mouse button over land, and the land around the pointer will be lowered in altitude, displayed by a darkening of the color or shade of the land.

Levels of terrain are displayed in shades. The lighter the shade, the higher the altitude. Each different shade represents a change of 500 meters. Since altitude is measured from sea level, and sea level can be anywhere—or nowhere—there is no exact altitude that can be assigned to each shade.

The cost for using the SET ALTITUDE tool to raise or lower the terrain is 50 E.U.

MOVING TOOL lets you pick any biome, niche, or civilization and move it. This can be useful for transplanting populations to other continents, or separating warring tribes. Since niches and biomes can occupy the same space in the display, you can use this tool to temporarily move the niche to see the biome that is displayed underneath it.

Click on the MOVING TOOL icon to activate it, then click and hold on a biome, niche or civilization. Drag the pointer to the destination location, and release the mouse button.

The cost for using the MOVING TOOL is 30 E.U.

 EXAMINE gives you information on individual spots in the DISPLAY AREA.

Click on the EXAMINE icon, and the mouse pointer changes to a magnifying glass. Then click and hold on a spot in the DISPLAY AREA. An information window will appear, giving you all the information that the simulation has about that spot.

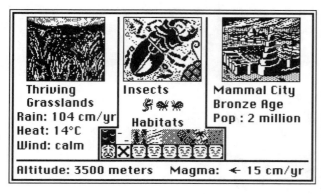

If you click and hold the button, and slowly drag the pointer across the screen, the information window will change and report on each section as you point to it.

The EXAMINE function is very useful for gathering information about specific areas of your planet. You will need this information for planning your next moves in planet development.

The same information window can be accessed by using the HELP function (hold the SHIFT KEY or HELP KEY while clicking on a spot) in the DISPLAY AREA.

The EXAMINE tool only gives information on places in the display window. For information on icons and tools, use the HELP function.

The cost for using the EXAMINE tool is 5 E.U.

There are four sections to the EXAMINE WINDOW: the Biome Section, the Life Section, the City Section, and the Altitude/Magma Section.

BIOME SECTION
The Biome Section shows a picture of the local biome (if any), and a description of its present condition, i.e., thriving, dying, etc. Next, it displays the rainfall, air temperature (heat), and wind direction.

If there is no biome present, this section will display the message "No Biome."

LIFE SECTION
If there is life, the Life Section shows a big picture of the predominant class of non-sentient life in that location. (Sentient life is treated separately in the City Section.) Below that are three small pictures. The middle one is the present species of the class, the left one is the species that it evolved from, and the right one is the species that, if all goes well, it will evolve into.

Below that is a chart of how that life class gets along in the various habitats, with a picture rating of how happy the species are there:

 Can't live there.

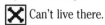 Can survive there, but it's miserable.

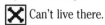 Can survive there, and quite nicely.

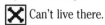 Paradise.

If there is no life, this section will display the message "No Life."

CITY SECTION

If there are no sapients near, this section will display the message "No Sapients."

If there are sapients, but no city, this section will display the message "Lightly Inhabited."

If there is a city, this section displays a large picture of the city, and tells the sapient class, the technology level, and the population.

ALTITUDE/MAGMA SECTION

This section, at the bottom of the window, displays this location's altitude and direction of magma flow.

CURRENT TOOL DISPLAY

The CURRENT TOOL DISPLAY shows the active icon, tool, life-form, biome, terraformer, or event, and the energy cost to use it.

DATA LAYER BUTTONS

These buttons control what data is displayed in the DISPLAY AREA. By clicking on these buttons, you toggle on and off the various layers of data. Using these buttons does not change the planet, or affect the model in any way—it only changes your view of the planet.

The default settings for these buttons changes with the Time Scale. In the Geologic Time Scale, the default setting has everything on except BIOMES and CITIES. In the Evolution Time Scale, everything is on except CITIES. In both the Civilization and Technology Time Scales, everything but LIFE defaults to the "on" setting.

OCEANS allows you to turn off and on the display of the Oceans, allowing you to see the elevation of the sea bottom.

BIOMES allows you to turn off and on the display of Biomes, so you can see the elevation of the terrain, and see Life and Cities more clearly.

CITIES allows you to turn off and on the display of the Cities of the current sentient species.

LIFE allows you to turn off and on the display of life-forms. Since these are so numerous and fast-moving, you may want to turn these off every so often to get a clearer view of the other things on your planet. This display is of individual species, not classes—there are 240 different species in SimEarth.

EVENTS allows you to turn off and on the display of Events.

CLIMATE OVERLAY BUTTONS

These buttons also control what data is displayed in the DISPLAY AREA. By clicking on these buttons, you toggle on and off the various layers of climate data. Using these buttons does not change the planet, or affect the model in any way—it only changes your view of the planet.

The default setting for all these buttons is OFF. Only one climate overlay can be active at any one time.

HEAT—A display of air temperature. Higher temperatures are represented by darker shades.

RAINFALL—A display of average rainfall. Higher rainfall densities are represented by darker shades.

WINDS—A display of the wind currents.

SEA FLOW—A display of the sea currents.

SEA HEAT—A display of water temperature. Higher temperatures are represented by darker shades.

MAGMA—A display of the magma currents under the planet's crust.

AVAILABLE ENERGY DISPLAY

This display lets you know how much energy you have left for planet manipulation and modification. The maximum energy that can be stored is set by the game level.

For a complete explanation, see the chapter "Energy."

The MAP WINDOW is your overview of the whole planet. It can be viewed as a flat or spherical projection.

MAP WINDOW

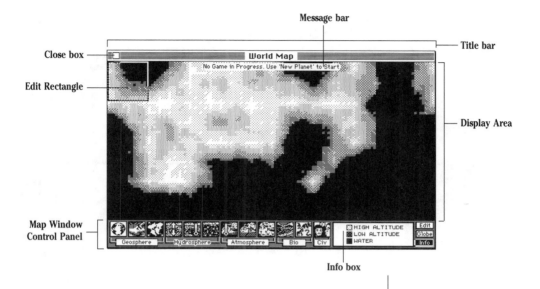

Message bar

Title bar

Close box

World Map

No Game in Progress. Use 'New Planet' to Start

Edit Rectangle

Display Area

Map Window
Control Panel

Geosphere   Hydrosphere   Atmosphere   Bio   Civ

⊠ HIGH ALTITUDE
⊠ LOW ALTITUDE
■ WATER

Edit
Globe
Info

Info box

The MAP WINDOW consists of three major parts: the TITLE BAR, the MAP DISPLAY AREA, and the CONTROL PANEL.

TITLE BAR
The TITLE BAR displays the type of map being shown in the MAP DISPLAY AREA and the date.

On the left side of the TITLE BAR is the CLOSE BOX. Clicking in this box will close the MAP WINDOW. You can bring the window back by selecting the MAP item in the WINDOWS MENU.

The MAP WINDOW can be moved on the screen by clicking and holding in the TITLE BAR, and dragging the window to its new location.

MAP WINDOW DISPLAY AREA
The MAP WINDOW DISPLAY AREA is where the map of the planet is displayed. There are many different types of displays and views of your planet, which are selected in the MAP WINDOW CONTROL PANEL.

In the MAP DISPLAY AREA you will see the EDIT RECTANGLE. This rectangle indicates the area of the world that is visible in the EDIT WINDOW. If you double-click in the EDIT RECTANGLE, the EDIT WINDOW will be brought to the front.

Messages from the simulation and the SimEarthlings sometimes appear at the top of the MAP DISPLAY AREA.

MAP WINDOW CONTROL PANEL

The MAP WINDOW CONTROL PANEL allows you to look at various views of your planet, giving different types of information in each view. From here you can also access all of the MODEL CONTROL PANELS, the HISTORY WINDOW, the EDIT WINDOW, and all the GRAPHS.

MAP DISPLAY ICONS

Along the top of the MAP WINDOW CONTROL PANEL, from the left, are 12 icons. Clicking on each of these icons displays different information in the MAP DISPLAY AREA. These 12 displays are divided into five groups: GEOSPHERE, HYDROSPHERE, ATMOSPHERE, BIO(SPHERE) and CIV(ILIZATION). A MODEL CONTROL PANEL can be accessed for four of the five groups (excluding HYDROSPHERE) by clicking on the name of that group.

GEOSPHERE GROUP

The GEOSPHERE group gives information on the terrain, events and magma flow of the planet. Clicking on the GEOSPHERE icon brings up the GEOSPHERE MODEL CONTROL PANEL.

TERRAIN MAP shows oceans and altitude across the planet. Higher altitudes are shown in lighter shades, lower altitudes are darker. Water is shown as either blue or black, depending on your monitor.

A legend of the altitude is visible in the INFO BOX near the right side of the MAP WINDOW CONTROL PANEL.

An extra feature accessed through this icon is a display of landmarks on the scenario planets. Click and hold on the icon, and names of landmarks will be displayed until you release the mouse button. This is available only on scenario planets. Random planets have no landmarks. Landmarks on Earth will stop being displayed 2,000,000 years in the future. We figure the names will change by then.

Double-clicking in this icon will open the GAIA WINDOW.

 GLOBAL EVENT MAP shows global events, such as hurricanes, forest fires, earthquakes, meteorites, wars, etc., as small symbols.

A key to the symbols is visible in the INFO BOX near the right of the CONTROL PANEL.

 CONTINENTAL DRIFT MAP shows the currents within the magma layer. Magma is the hot molten rock within the earth, upon which the continental plates are "floating." The currents here determine the direction and speed of continental drift.

A legend of the magma current vectors is available for this map in the INFO BOX.

HYDROSPHERE GROUP
This group gives information on the ocean. There is no MODEL CONTROL PANEL for the Hydrosphere.

 HIDE/SHOW OCEANS toggles the ocean display on and off so you can see the elevation of the ocean floor. This doesn't make the ocean go away—it just makes it invisible. This option is used in combination with other maps, and has no legend in the INFO BOX.

 OCEAN TEMPERATURE displays the average annual ocean temperature. In most cases this will correspond closely with the air temperature, but it will change much more slowly.

The INFO BOX can display both a legend to the ocean temperatures and a graph of average ocean temperature over time. To switch between these two displays, click on the INFO BUTTON in the lower-right corner of the MAP WINDOW CONTROL PANEL.

 OCEAN CURRENTS displays the surface currents of the oceans.

A legend of ocean current vectors is available for this map in the INFO BOX.

ATMOSPHERE GROUP
This group displays information on the atmosphere and climate. Clicking on the ATMOSPHERE icon brings up the ATMOSPHERE MODEL CONTROL PANEL.

 AIR TEMPERATURE displays the average annual air temperature. The heat displayed here comes primarily from the sun, and secondarily from warm ocean areas.

The INFO BOX can display both a legend of the air temperatures and a graph of average air temperature over time. To switch between these two displays, click on the INFO BUTTON in the lower-right corner of the MAP WINDOW CONTROL PANEL.

Double-clicking on this icon will open the ATMOSPHERIC COMPOSITION GRAPH.

 RAINFALL displays the average yearly rainfall. The heaviest rainfall will usually be concentrated over the equator.

The INFO BOX can display both a legend for the rainfall map and a graph of average rainfall over time. To switch between these two displays, click on the INFO BUTTON in the lower-right corner of the MAP WINDOW CONTROL PANEL.

Double-clicking on this icon will open the ATMOSPHERIC COMPOSITION GRAPH.

AIR CURRENTS shows the average air currents. As with ocean currents, these are determined by thermal disequilibrium and Coriolis effect.

A key to the air current vectors is available in the INFO BOX.

Double-clicking on this icon will open the ATMOSPHERIC COMPOSITION GRAPH.

BIOSPHERE GROUP
This group gives information on the life on your planet. Clicking on the Biosphere icon brings up the BIOSPHERE MODEL CONTROL PANEL.

BIOMES displays the distribution of biomes on your planet.

The INFO BOX can display both a legend to biome distribution on the map and a graph of average biomass over time. To switch between these two displays, click on the INFO BUTTON in the lower-right corner of the MAP WINDOW CONTROL PANEL.

Double-clicking on this icon opens the BIOME RATIO GRAPH.

LIFE displays the diversity of life on your planet.

The INFO BOX can display both a legend to the life-forms and a graph of genetic diversity over time. To switch between these two displays, click on the INFO BUTTON in the lower-right corner of the MAP WINDOW CONTROL PANEL.

Double-clicking on this icon will open the LIFE CLASS RATIO GRAPH.

CIVILIZATION GROUP
This is where you will find worldwide information on civilizations on your planet. Clicking on the Civilization icon brings up the CIVILIZATION MODEL CONTROL PANEL.

Bio

Civ

 CIVILIZATION shows the distribution of civilizations on the planet. More advanced civilizations will appear darker. Terraformers will be shown on this map in black.

The INFO BOX can display both a legend to the civilizations on the planet and a graph of the population of your sentient species over time. To switch between these two displays, click on the INFO BUTTON in the lower-right corner of the MAP WINDOW CONTROL PANEL.

Double-clicking on this icon will open the TECHNOLOGY RATIO GRAPH.

INFO BOX

The INFO BOX is located just to the right of the Civilization icon.

This box displays helpful information about the map view: legends to help interpret the map, and graphs of the information displayed in the map shown over time. These graphs correspond with the graphs in the HISTORY WINDOW.

You can bring up the HISTORY WINDOW by double-clicking inside the INFO BOX.

Some map views have map legends to be displayed here, others have both legends and graphs. HIDE/SHOW OCEANS has neither. Toggle between info sets by clicking on the INFO BUTTON in the lower-right corner of the MAP WINDOW.

ACTIVE MAP ICON	INFO BUTTON HIGHLIGHTED	INFO BUTTON NOT HIGHLIGHTED
TERRAIN MAP	HIGH ALTITUDE / LOW ALTITUDE / WATER	HIGH ALTITUDE / LOW ALTITUDE / WATER
GLOBAL EVENTS*	Hurricane / Wave / Quake / Meteor / Nuke / Plague / Volcano / Fire / War *	Hurricane / Wave / Quake / Meteor / Nuke / Plague / Volcano / Fire / War *
CONTINENTAL DRIFT	Current Vectors	Current Vectors
HIDE/SHOW OCEANS	N/A	N/A
OCEAN TEMP	>50° / 25-50° / 0-25° / <0° °C	Sea Temperature
OCEAN CURRENTS	Current Vectors	Current Vectors
AIR TEMPERATURE	>50° / 25-50° / 0-25° / <0° °C	Air Temperature
RAINFALL	>150 / 50-150 / 10-50 / <10 cm/year	BioMass
AIR CURRENTS	Current Vectors	Current Vectors
BIOMES		BioMass
LIFE		Diversity
CIVILIZATION		Population

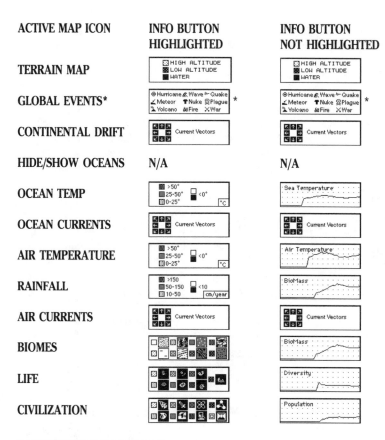

* Note: Two Events, Pollution and Exodus, are not included in the Event Map legend, but will appear on the map when they occur.

DAISYWORLD INFO DISPLAY

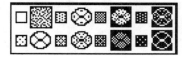

When in the Daisyworld Scenario, in the Biome view, the highlighted INFO BOX displays the distribution of the different shades of daisies.

CONTINENTAL DRIFT RECORD

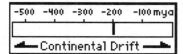

-500 -400 -300 -200 -100 mya

◀— Continental Drift —▶

If you click and hold on the INFO BOX (regardless of the status of the INFO BUTTON) and slowly move the mouse back and forth, you will be shown an animated history of continental drift on your planet.

BUTTONS

There are three buttons on the far right side of the MAP CONTROL PANEL.

Edit

EDIT brings the EDIT WINDOW to the front.

Globe

GLOBE changes the MAP WINDOW view from a flat robinson projection to a spherically mapped globe projection. All maps and displays are available in GLOBE mode—the MAP WINDOW CONTROL PANEL doesn't change. When in this mode, the GLOBE BUTTON will be highlighted. Clicking on the GLOBE BUTTON again will return you to the flat projection.

The EDIT RECTANGLE becomes an EDIT TRAPEZOID on the GLOBE. If you double-click in the EDIT TRAPEZOID, the EDIT WINDOW will be brought to the front.

Clicking, holding, and dragging the outer rim of the globe will allow you to move it on the screen.

The interior of the globe can be viewed by double-clicking on the globe, anywhere but in the EDIT TRAPEZOID. Click again to return to the surface of the planet.

Info

INFO toggles between different information views in the INFO BOX.

ACCESSING MODEL CONTROL PANELS

The MODEL CONTROL PANELS are available through the MODELS MENU, but they can also be accessed by clicking on the icons GEOSPHERE, ATMOSPHERE, BIOSPHERE, and CIVILIZATION on the MAP CONTROL PANEL.

Geosphere   Atmosphere   Bio   Civ

ACCESSING GRAPHS

All graphs can be accessed both through the GRAPHS MENU and the MAP CONTROL PANEL. They are opened by double-clicking on various icons in the MAP CONTROL PANEL.

The ATMOSPHERIC COMPOSITION GRAPH is opened by double-clicking on any of the three ATMOSPHERE icons.

The BIOME RATIO GRAPH is opened by double-clicking on the BIOMES icon.

The LIFE CLASS RATIO GRAPH is opened by double-clicking on the LIFE icon.

The TECHNOLOGY RATIO GRAPH is opened by double-clicking on the CIVILIZATION icon.

ACCESSING OTHER WINDOWS

Double-click in the INFO BOX to open the HISTORY WINDOW.

Double-click on the TERRAIN MAP icon to open the GAIA WINDOW.

ACCESS TO GRAPHS AND WINDOWS
FROM MAP WINDOW CONTROL PANEL

—— A single line represents a single click.

=== A double line represents a double-click.

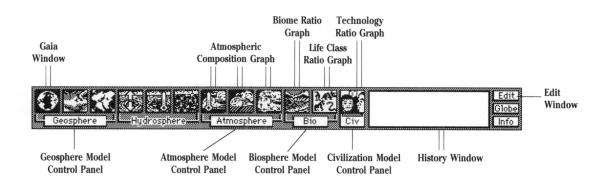

GAIA WINDOW

The GAIA WINDOW shows Gaia, a caricature of the Earth as one living organism. This "face of the planet" will give you constant feedback on the planet's "mood."

This window can be opened by selecting GAIA from the WINDOWS MENU, or by double-clicking on the TERRAIN MAP icon in the MAP WINDOW.

The planet's mood is based on how well life on the planet is doing. The face will be asleep until life forms, then it will wake up. The moods range from bliss to horror. Everything that happens and everything you do affects the face.

At the bottom of this window is a little message bar that will display messages from Gaia. In the upper-right corner of the window is the Sun. As solar heat increases through time, the Sun will slowly begin to enlarge. At the end of your planet's 10-billion-year life, the Sun will burn up Gaia.

You may want to keep this window in a corner of the screen, and let it guide you as you develop your planet.

Its eyes will follow the pointer around the screen. Please don't poke it in the eye.

The HISTORY WINDOW provides a graphical record of many factors that define your planet.

HISTORY WINDOW

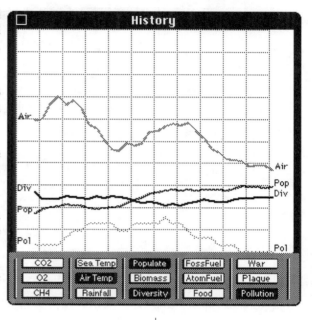

Use this window for tracking the changes and development of your planet's chemical composition, temperature, humidity, life, events, and pollution.

This window is accessed through the WINDOWS MENU, and by double-clicking on the INFO BOX in the MAP WINDOW CONTROL PANEL.

Click on any of the icons at the bottom of the window to toggle the display of that factor on and off.

There are 15 items that can be displayed as a graph in this window. Up to four items can be displayed at a time.

CO_2 displays Carbon Dioxide levels in the atmosphere.

O_2 displays Oxygen levels in the atmosphere.

CH_4 displays Methane levels in the atmosphere.

SEA TEMPERATURE displays overall average temperature of the oceans.

AIR TEMPERATURE displays overall average temperature of the atmosphere.

RAINFALL displays overall average planetary rainfall.

POPULATION displays population of the sentient species on your planet.

BIOMASS displays the total weight of all plant and animal matter on the planet. The biomass of Earth is 99% plant material.

DIVERSITY displays the number of different species of life on the planet. Major extinctions will be visible here.

FOSSIL FUELS displays the amount of fossil fuel reserves still within the planet. This amount grows during the Evolution Time Scale as biomass decays, and is depleted by civilization.

ATOMIC FUEL displays the amount of atomic fuel reserves within the planet.

FOOD displays the total amount of food produced on the planet.

WAR displays the level of armed conflict across the planet.

PLAGUE displays the number of plague events that have occurred.

POLLUTION displays the total amount of toxic releases by the sentient species.

To keep the planet data file at a reasonable size, a complete history is not saved with the planet. Once the graph goes off the left of the HISTORY WINDOW it is lost forever.

There will be a dividing line to mark when one Time Scale ends and another begins.

The amount of time displayed per division in this window is different for each of the Time Scales. The full width of the HISTORY WINDOW covers approximately:
    1,000,000,000 years in the Geologic Time Scale;
    70,000,000 years in the Evolution Time Scale;
    2,500 years in the Civilization Time Scale; and
    50 years in the Technology Time Scale.

REPORT WINDOW

The REPORT WINDOW is your main source of feedback on how well both you and life on your planet are doing. The information in the REPORT WINDOW changes for the various Time Scales, giving information that is useful for each era. There is also a special REPORT WINDOW for the Daisyworld Scenario.

REPORT WINDOW
IN THE GEOLOGIC TIME SCALE
In this Time Scale, the REPORT WINDOW gives four items of information.

VIABILITY
This rating tells you how hospitable your world is to multi-celled animals. Viability is based on the oxygen and dust content of the atmosphere. The rating levels are:

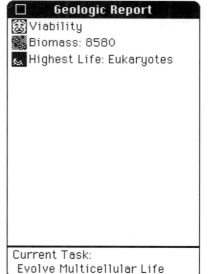

Life cannot exist here.

Life can exist, but barely.

Life can exist fairly well.

Paradise.

BIOMASS
Biomass is the total weight of all plants and animals on the planet. In the Geologic Time Scale there are no plants, so the Biomass is formed entirely of Eukaryotes. The theoretical maximum value for Biomass in this Time Scale is 40,960.

HIGHEST LIFE
This is a display of the most advanced microbe life-form.

CURRENT TASK
Your CURRENT TASK is what needs to be accomplished before moving on to the next Time Scale.

REPORT WINDOW
IN THE EVOLUTION TIME SCALE

In this Time Scale, the REPORT WINDOW gives a few more items of information.

```
┌──────────────────────────────┐
│ ☐     Evolution Report        │
├──────────────────────────────┤
│  No Civilization Present.     │
├──────────────────────────────┤
│            -Highest-          │
│  -IQ-      -Intelligence-     │
│                               │
│   36    ▨ 1st: Radiate        │
│   18    ▥ 2nd: Arthropod      │
│    6    ▤ 3rd: Mollusk        │
├──────────────────────────────┤
│  ⁻_ Biomass: 8279             │
│  ▨ Viability                  │
│  ▨ Growth                     │
│                               │
│                               │
│                               │
│                               │
├──────────────────────────────┤
│  Current Task:                │
│  Discover Fire                │
└──────────────────────────────┘
```

INTELLIGENCE

This is a display of the "race to intelligence." The three most advanced forms of life are listed, and given an "intelligence" rating (IQ). This rating is just a rough estimate of how advanced the life-forms are and does not relate to human IQ levels.

This display show the leaders in the race to sentience. When a life-form reaches an IQ of 100, it becomes sentient.

BIOMASS

Biomass in the Evolution Time Scale consists of the combined mass of both the animal life and the biomes—plant life. Jungles are the richest, highest mass biomes, Deserts the poorest and lowest mass. The theoretical maximum value for biomass is 180,224.

The icon shown for Biomass is the predominant biome.

VIABILITY

This rating tells you how hospitable your world is to multi-celled animals. Viability is based on the oxygen and dust content of the atmosphere. The rating levels are the same as in the Geologic REPORT WINDOW.

GROWTH

The biomass requires CO_2 for survival and growth. The Growth rating is based on the CO_2 content of the atmosphere.

CURRENT TASK

Your CURRENT TASK is what needs to be accomplished before moving on to the next Time Scale.

REPORT WINDOW IN THE CIVILIZATION AND TECHNOLOGY TIME SCALES

In these Time Scales, you are given much more information.

SENTIENT TYPE
This tells you what class of life is the dominant, intelligent species on your planet.

HIGHEST TECHNOLOGY
tells you the highest level of civilization on your planet.

MEDIAN TECHNOLOGY
tells you the average technology level of your planet.

POPULATION
tells the current population of your planet's sentient species.

LIFE QUALITY
gives an overall "quality of life" rating for the sentient species on your planet. The two factors taken into consideration in this rating are number of work hours per week, and your allocation of resources to Arts and Media. It is difficult to have a life quality above tolerable in lower technology levels.

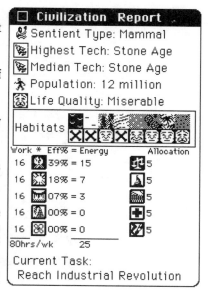

The possible quality levels are: Heavenly, Marvelous, Good, Pleasant, Tolerable, Unpleasant, Bad, Miserable, and Hellish.

HABITATS
shows the ability of your sentient species to survive in the various biomes, and how well they are adapted to the habitat. The rating levels are:

Can't live there at all.

Can live there, but hates it.

Can live there, and likes it.

Paradise.

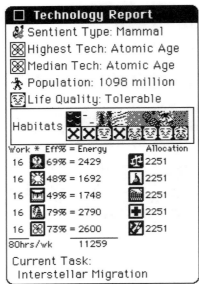

ENERGY SECTION

Below the Habitats is a large section that deals with energy. To best understand what happens here, look at the REPORT WINDOW and the CIVILIZATION MODEL CONTROL PANEL side-by-side.

WORK is the amount of hours per week that your sentient SimEarthlings must work to survive. In SimEarth, we have simplified the concept of work: all work produces energy.

The amount of time intelligent SimEarthlings work is divided between five different energy sources. The amount of time worked to produce energy from each of the five sources is set on the left side of the CIVILIZATION MODEL CONTROL PANEL. The total number of hours worked per week affects the quality of life.

TYPES OF ENERGY

BIOENERGY—Burning wood, animal power, plant power (farming), work done by hand by the sentient species.

SOLAR/WIND—Sun-drying of food and clothes, windmills, sailing ships, solar heating, wind-powered generators, solar electric cells, satellites collecting solar energy.

HYDRO/GEO—Waterwheels, dams, steam power, hydroelectric power, geothermal power.

FOSSIL FUEL—Coal and oil made from long-dead animals.

NUCLEAR—Atomic power plants.

EFFICIENCY is a rating of how much energy you receive for the amount of work put in. The efficiency of each energy source varies with the level of technology.

ENERGY EFFICIENCY VS. TECHNOLOGY LEVEL

	Bioenergy	Solar/Wind	Hydro/Geo	Fossil Fuel	Nuclear
Stone Age	40%	20%	10%	0%	0%
Bronze Age	40%	20%	30%	10%	0%
Iron Age	60%	20%	30%	30%	0%
Industrial Age	60%	30%	50%	80%	10%
Atomic Age	70%	50%	50%	80%	80%
Information Age	80%	60%	60%	90%	90%
Nanotech Age	90%	80%	80%	90%	90%

The efficiency rating displayed and used in the REPORT WINDOW is averaged over the number of the various technologies. For example, if your planet has one city in the Nanotech Age, and one city in the Stone Age, then the displayed efficiency rating for Atomic Energy would be 45% (1 city * 90% + 1 city * 0% / 2 cities).

This rating can be changed by the availability of resources. As fossil fuel and atomic fuel run out, their efficiency rating declines to 0%.

ENERGY is the amount of each type of energy produced, with a total for all combined energy sources.

All energy that is produced is used. The total energy produced will roughly equal the total of all the allocated energy. There is some energy lost, and some rounding off of numbers for the display, but it all gets used.

ALLOCATION is what your sentients are doing with the energy. All the energy produced is allocated and used. Allocation is set on the right side of the CIVILIZATION MODEL CONTROL PANEL.

The possible uses that you can allocate energy to are:

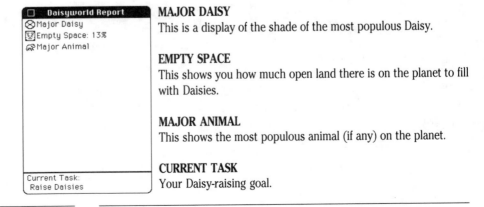

PHILOSOPHY—Philosophy is a deterrent to war. Investing in philosophy reduces the number and intensity of violent conflicts on your planet.

SCIENCE—Investing in science helps your civilizations advance to higher technology levels. You must have at least some investment in science to advance at all. Advancing technology levels too fast, or without a fair share of philosophy, agriculture, medicine, and art/media does not produce a stable, long-lasting civilization. If you invest too much too soon in science, your population will die off from war and plague.

AGRICULTURE—Investing in agriculture increases food production, which increases the rate of population growth of your sentient species.

MEDICINE—Investment in medicine reduces the number and severity of plagues.

ART/MEDIA—Investment in art/media improves the quality of life of your SimEarthling global citizen.

CURRENT TASK tells you what needs to be accomplished to advance to the next Time Scale.

REPORT WINDOW
IN THE DAISYWORLD SCENARIO

In the Daisyworld Scenario, you are only given four items of information.

```
┌─────────────────────────┐
│ □  Daisyworld Report    │
│⊗Major Daisy             │
│😟Empty Space: 13%        │
│🐾Major Animal           │
│                         │
│                         │
│                         │
│                         │
│                         │
│                         │
│                         │
│                         │
├─────────────────────────┤
│ Current Task:           │
│  Raise Daisies          │
└─────────────────────────┘
```

MAJOR DAISY
This is a display of the shade of the most populous Daisy.

EMPTY SPACE
This shows you how much open land there is on the planet to fill with Daisies.

MAJOR ANIMAL
This shows the most populous animal (if any) on the planet.

CURRENT TASK
Your Daisy-raising goal.

REPORT WINDOW
IN THE TERRAFORMING SCENARIOS

In the Terraforming Scenarios, Mars and Venus, you are given much of the same information as in the CIVILIZATION and TECHNOLOGY REPORT WINDOWS, but with added terraforming progress feedback.

VIABILITY

This rating tells you how hospitable your world is to life. Viability is based on the oxygen and dust content of the atmosphere. The rating levels are the same as in the GEOLOGICAL, CIVILIZATION, and TECHNOLOGY REPORT WINDOWS.

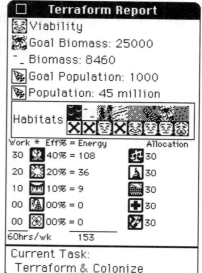

GOAL BIOMASS

This is the biomass that you must attain before the planet is considered terraformed.

BIOMASS

This is your world's present biomass. The icon shown for Biomass is the predominant biome.

GOAL POPULATION

This is the population your planet must reach to be considered colonized.

POPULATION

This is your present population.

HABITAT AND ENERGY

The HABITAT and ENERGY sections of this window are the same as in the CIVILIZATION and TECHNOLOGY REPORT WINDOWS, with two exceptions:

   These sections will not appear in the window until you have begun the colonization process (placing sentient life on the planet).

   The HABITAT section will always display the information for sentient mammals since the majority of SimEarth players are mammals.

CURRENT TASK

Your current task is to terraform and colonize the planet.

TUTORIAL WINDOW

The TUTORIAL WINDOW is a text window that gives a brief review of the tutorial in this manual. It can be accessed through the WINDOWS MENU.

Like all help and text windows in SimEarth, it can be moved around the screen and re-sized. Click on the up and down arrows in the Scroll Bar on the right side of the window to scroll through the text.

Depending on your computer, you may or may not be able to have this window open at the same time as the HELP WINDOW.

```
═╪□════════════  Help: SimEarth Tutorial  ═════
   Welcome to SimEarth:The Living Planet. This
 window will give you a brief introduction to
 SimEarth and walk you through some of the basic
 functions.
   Help screens such as this are available for
 almost every control, menu and button. To open
 the help window hold down the shift key and then
 click on the control, menu or button that you want
 information about.
```

GLOSSARY WINDOW

The GLOSSARY WINDOW is a special HELP WINDOW that can be accessed through the WINDOWS MENU. It gives definitions for words and terms that are used in the SimEarth program.

Like all help and text windows in SimEarth, it can be moved around the screen and re-sized. Click on the up and down arrows on the right side of the window to scroll through the text.

```
═╪□════════════  Help: Glossary  ═════
  Aerobic- Requires oxygen. This can apply to animals,
 machines or processes.
  Air Pressure- The pressure caused by air molecules
 bouncing against a surface.  Vacuum has no air
 pressure.
  Albedo- The reflectivity of a surface. A surface
 with high albedo will reflect sunlight.  A surface with
 low albedo will absorb sunlight.  Snow (high albedo)
 reflects sunlight and remains cold.
  Anaerobic- Does not require oxygen.  This can apply
 to animals, machines or processes.
```

GRAPHS

There are four graph windows, which can be opened through the GRAPHS MENU and through the MAP WINDOW icons. Only one GRAPH WINDOW can be displayed at a time.

These windows can be moved around the screen by clicking and dragging the TITLE BAR, and closed by clicking the CLOSE BOX.

Two of the graphs display their information over time as well as for the present. The information is given in horizontal or vertical bars, with the most current bar in front.

ATMOSPHERIC COMPOSITION GRAPH

This graph is accessed either through the AIR SAMPLE item on the GRAPHS MENU or by double-clicking on the AIR TEMPERATURE icon on the MAP WINDOW CONTROL PANEL.

The ATMOSPHERIC COMPOSITION GRAPH gives only the atmospheric composition for the present time. Its information is shown in horizontal bars.

It displays the chemical composition of your planet's atmosphere. It gives the ratio in percentages of four gases—Nitrogen (N_2), Oxygen (O_2), Carbon Dioxide (CO_2), and Methane (CH_4)—plus dust particles and water vapor (H_2O). It also gives the air pressure expressed in atmospheres.

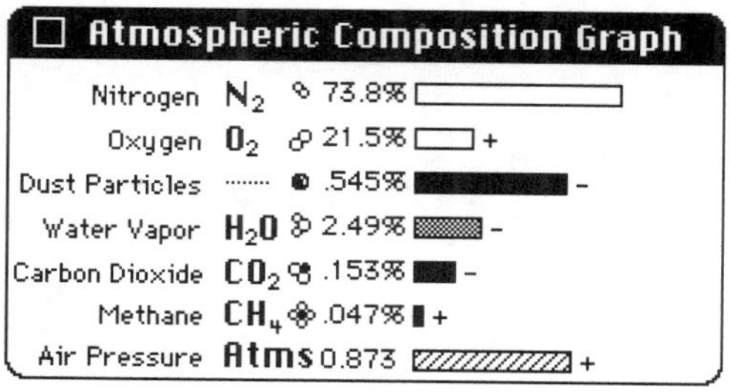

☐ **Atmospheric Composition Graph**

Nitrogen	N_2	◈ 73.8%	☐
Oxygen	O_2	♂ 21.5%	☐ +
Dust Particles	⋯⋯	● .545%	▓▓
Water Vapor	H_2O	◈ 2.49%	▓ −
Carbon Dioxide	CO_2	◈ .153%	▓ −
Methane	CH_4	✦ .047%	▌ +
Air Pressure	**Atms**	0.873	▨▨▨▨ +

The plusses and minuses at the end of the bars indicate whether that item is increasing or decreasing. If there is no plus or minus after the bar, the level is temporarily stable.

The shade or pattern of the bars is a scale indication.
�■ Percentage is less than 1%.
▓▓ Percentage is between 1 and 10%.
☐ Percentage is above 10%.
The Air Pressure bar has its own shade, and does not change with the percentage.

This graph is useful for monitoring trends in atmospheric composition:

Too little oxygen, and life will end.
Too much oxygen, and fires will burn all over the planet.
Too little carbon dioxide, and plants will die.

Too much carbon dioxide, and animals will become extinct.
Too much dust causes solar blockage and extinctions.
Water vapor affects rainfall.
Water vapor, carbon dioxide and methane are greenhouse gases—high levels
will increase the greenhouse warming effect.

BIOME RATIO GRAPH

This graph is accessed either through the BIOMES item on the GRAPHS MENU
or by double-clicking on the BIOMES icon on the MAP WINDOW CONTROL
PANEL.

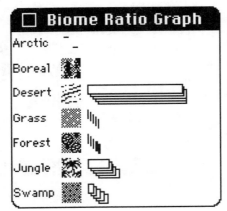

It displays the relative amounts of the seven biomes on
your planet over time.

This graph is useful for detecting and tracking trends in
the dominant biomes.

When playing the Daisyworld Scenario, the BIOME
RATIO GRAPH displays the eight shades of daisies.

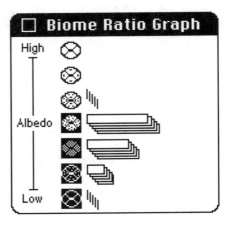

This graph is accessed either through the LIFE-FORMS item on the GRAPHS MENU or by double-clicking on the LIFE icon on the MAP WINDOW CONTROL PANEL.

LIFE CLASS RATIO GRAPH

It displays the relative amounts of the life classes on your planet over time. The 14 classes from the PLACE LIFE tool are displayed, plus the Carnifern: a mobile carnivorous plant that can achieve sentience.

This graph is useful for tracking trends in the life on your planet.

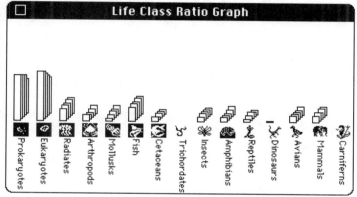

This graph is accessed either through the TECHNOLOGY item on the GRAPHS MENU or by double-clicking on the CIVILIZATION icon on the MAP WINDOW CONTROL PANEL.

TECHNOLOGY RATIO GRAPH

It displays the population ratio between the various levels of civilization on your planet.

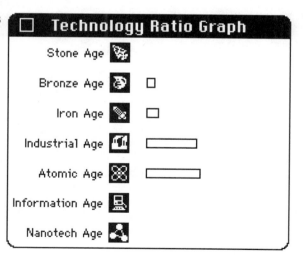

MODEL CONTROL PANELS

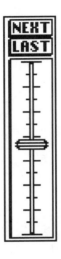

The four MODEL CONTROL PANELS are used to observe and change the settings of many variables in the model. These CONTROL PANELS are the only places in SimEarth that are used only for INPUT.

These windows are reached either through the MODELS MENU or through the MAP WINDOW CONTROL PANEL.

Only one MODEL CONTROL PANEL can be displayed at a time. You can cycle through the four panels forward or backward by clicking on the NEXT and LAST buttons in the upper-right corner.

There are 16 possible settings for each item on each control panel.

To change model settings, first click on the item you want to change. The name of the item and an indicator (usually an arrow) will become highlighted. A dotted box will appear around the indicator. Both the indicator and the SLIDER CONTROL at the right of the panel will display the setting of the active item.

Next, click on the SLIDER CONTROL above or below the slider to increase or decrease the setting one increment. You can also click and drag the slider to change settings.

Even though the life on your planet is self-regulating, and affects the model, these changes are not shown on the MODEL CONTROL PANELS. These panels reflect your settings and display only your changes.

There will be a lag between the time you change a MODEL CONTROL PANEL and the time your change takes effect.

The cost in energy for changing the control panels is 30 E.U. per click and 150 E.U. per drag. For small changes, use clicks. For big changes use drags.

If you change a panel from the lowest to the highest setting by clicking, it will cost you 30 E.U. X 15 clicks = 450 E.U. The same change by dragging would cost 150 E.U. You would save a lot of energy by dragging instead of clicking.

If you change a panel setting one level, clicking would cost you 30 E.U., but dragging would still cost 150 E.U.

GEOSPHERE MODEL CONTROL PANEL

This MODEL CONTROL PANEL deals with the variable factors affecting the Geosphere, Meteor Impacts, and the Axial Tilt of your planet.

It can be accessed through the MODELS MENU or by clicking on the GEOSPHERE icon in the MAP WINDOW CONTROL PANEL.

The factors you can adjust are:

VOLCANIC ACTIVITY controls the frequency of periodic volcanic eruptions. In early stages of the planet this will influence the formation of continental areas.

EROSION controls the rate of "smoothing" of the terrain by erosion. Increasing erosion also increases CO_2 in the atmosphere.

CONTINENTAL DRIFT controls the rate at which the continents move on the magma layer.

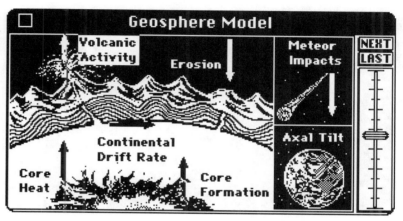

CORE HEAT controls the temperature of the planet's core. The higher the core heat, the larger and more severe the volcanos. Also, the hotter the core, the more the direction of magma flow will change.

CORE FORMATION controls the rate at which the planetary core forms. As the core forms, it gets larger. The size of the core affects the speed at which the magma flows. The bigger the core, the slower the magma. The slower the magma, the smaller the volcanos, and the slower the continental drift.

METEOR IMPACT controls the frequency of periodic meteor (or planetesimal) strikes.

AXIAL TILT controls the tilt of your planet's spin axis. This affects the severity of the seasons—the greater the tilt, the greater the seasonal severity. This is only noticeable in the two modern Time Scales. The current tilt of the real Earth's axis is about 22 degrees from vertical.

ATMOSPHERE MODEL CONTROL PANEL

Atmosphere

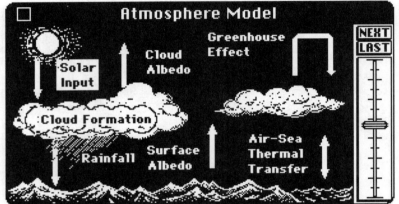

This MODEL CONTROL PANEL deals with the variable factors affecting the atmosphere of your planet.

It can be accessed through the MODELS MENU or by clicking on the ATMOSPHERE icon in the MAP WINDOW CONTROL PANEL.

The factors you can adjust are:

SOLAR INPUT controls the incoming solar radiation (heat). This is the amount of heat from the Sun that hits your planet. Setting the slider all the way down will turn the sun off.

CLOUD ALBEDO controls the reflectivity of the clouds, which controls the amount of sunlight (heat) that passes through them to the planet.

GREENHOUSE EFFECT controls the intensity of the warming greenhouse effect. The greenhouse effect is caused by certain gases that block outgoing infrared radiation. In SimEarth, the greenhouse gases are water vapor (H_2O), methane (CH_4), and carbon dioxide (CO_2).

CLOUD FORMATION controls the amount of clouds formed from a given amount of evaporation.

RAINFALL controls the amount of rainfall on the planet.

SURFACE ALBEDO controls the reflectivity of surface biomes. The higher the albedo, the more solar radiation is reflected back into space.

AIR-SEA THERMAL TRANSFER controls the rate at which the air and ocean can exchange heat.

This MODEL CONTROL PANEL deals with the variable factors affecting the biosphere of your planet.

It can be accessed through the MODELS MENU or by clicking on the BIOSPHERE icon in the MAP WINDOW CONTROL PANEL.

The factors you can adjust are:

THERMAL TOLERANCE controls the temperature range in which life can survive. The higher the setting, the wider the acceptable temperature range for life.

REPRODUCTION RATE controls how quickly life as a whole will reproduce.

CO_2 ABSORPTION controls how much carbon dioxide is scrubbed from the air by the plants.

BIOSPHERE MODEL CONTROL PANEL

Bio

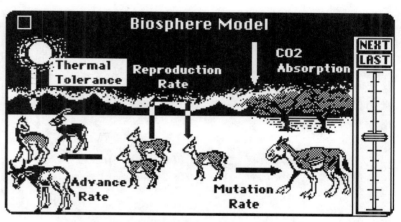

ADVANCE RATE controls the rate at which life-forms advance to the next higher level of development towards intelligence. It is usually a change of one species.

MUTATION RATE controls the rate at which life-forms will mutate. Mutations can jump ahead, skipping species, to the next class of life.

CIVILIZATION MODEL CONTROL PANEL

This panel is used to define and control the civilized, sentient species on your planet. It is only useful in the Civilization and Technology Time Scales.

It can be accessed through the MODELS MENU or by clicking on the CIVILIZATION icon in the MAP WINDOW CONTROL PANEL.

The CIVILIZATION MODEL CONTROL PANEL is one of the real challenges of SimEarth. You must make some important decisions and set priorities both for the types of energies you want to invest in and the uses you want to put the energy to.

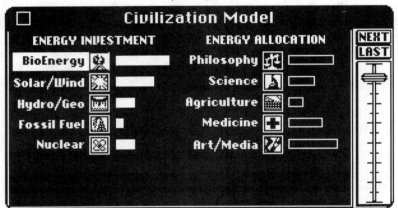

This control panel has a major effect on the REPORT WINDOW. It is a good idea to have these two on the screen together.

ENERGY INVESTMENT
The left side of the control panel is where you set your priorities for investment in various types of energies.

The greater your priority, the longer you should make the bar next to the choice. If you don't want to invest in a particular type of energy at all, then shrink the bar to nothing.

The total amount of investment in all the types of energy sets the amount of hours your global citizen must work per week. The work week is a major factor affecting quality of life.

The types of energy you can invest in are:

BIOENERGY—Burning wood, animal power, plant power (farming), work done by hand by the sentient species.

SOLAR/WIND—Sun-drying of food and clothes, windmills, sailing ships, solar heating, wind-powered generators, solar electric cells, satellites collecting solar energy.

HYDRO/GEO—Waterwheels, dams, steam power, hydroelectric power, geothermal power.

FOSSIL FUEL—Coal made from long-dead animals.

 NUCLEAR—Atomic reactors, bombs, etc.

ENERGY ALLOCATION

The right side of the control panel is where you allocate the energy. All energy produced is used.

Rather than actual numerical settings, allocations are ratios. This means that you should adjust the length of the bars for each allocation choice to show your priorities—the longer the bar, the higher the priority.

If all the bars are all the way up, or all are in the middle, the model interprets your settings the same. It is the differences in lengths that matters, not the actual length.

It is best not to turn any of the settings all the way off. The allocation setting has a feedback effect on the energy investment. Low allocations can reduce the efficiency at which technologies can produce the energy. This can make your technology level decline.

The uses to which you can put your energy are:

PHILOSOPHY—Philosophy is a deterrent to war. Investing in philosophy reduces the number and intensity of violent conflicts on your planet.

SCIENCE—Investing in science helps your civilizations advance to higher technology levels. You must have at least some investment in science to advance at all. Advancing technology levels too fast, or without a fair share of philosophy, agriculture, medicine, and art/media does not produce a stable, long-lasting civilization. If you invest too much too soon in science, your population will die off from war and plague.

AGRICULTURE—Investing in agriculture increases food production, which increases the rate of population growth of your sentient species.

MEDICINE—Investment in medicine reduces the number and severity of plagues.

ART/MEDIA—Investment in art/media improves the quality of life of your SimEarthling global citizen.

SimEarth

TIME SCALES

INTRODUCTION TO TIME SCALES

SimEarth runs in four different Time Scales: Geologic, Evolution, Civilization and Technology. Each Time Scale simulates a different set of factors on the planet. You can start a planet at any Time Scale, or start at the first (Geologic) and the game will automatically evolve through all the Time Scales.

In the Civilization and Technology Time Scales, you can rush the intelligent SimEarthling's advance through the levels of civilizations by model manipulation or by using the Monolith.

Advancing too fast is not necessarily a good thing. If you do not allow enough time in the Geologic and Evolution Time Scales, there won't be enough fossil fuel for the later Time Scales. You will need a wide population base for continued advancement. If you push a small group to advance before its population has built up, it will stagnate and die out.

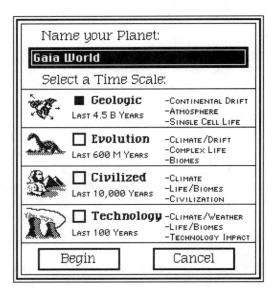

GEOLOGIC TIME SCALE

The Geologic Time Scale begins just after a planet is formed and begins cooling. It ends with the development of multi-celled life. This covers the time period on the real Earth from 4.5 billion to 570 million years ago.

In this Time Scale, the planet changes very slowly, so the simulation time is sped up to keep things moving. The Time/Simulation cycle for this Time Scale is 10 million years. This means that each time the program runs through one simulation cycle, 10 million years passes on the planet.

Your available energy builds up at 1 E.U. per Time/Simulation cycle.

The factors simulated in this Time Scale, in order of their influence, are: continental drift, atmospheric composition, extraterrestrial collisions, single-celled life, and climate.

The goal of this Time Scale is to manipulate all the simulated factors to facilitate the formation of multicellular life, at which time you will be advanced to the next and slower Time Scale, Evolution.

Time moves very fast in this Time Scale, and your planet only has 10 billion years to live. If you want to complete all the Time Scales before the end of your planet, you should try to reach the next Time Scale when your planet is between three and four billion years old. Don't advance too soon, or there will not be enough fossil fuels for later civilizations.

SUMMARY—GEOLOGIC TIME SCALE

Time/Simulation cycle	10 million years
Energy increase/cycle	1 E.U.
Time on real Earth	4.5 to .570 billion years ago
Factors simulated	Continental drift
	Atmospheric composition
	Extraterrestrial collisions
	Single-celled life
	Climate
Advancement conditions	Evolution of multicellular organisms
Optimum advancement age	Between 3 and 4 billion years

THINGS TO DO:

Design continents.

Spell your name in land masses.

Burn off oceans.

Make life impossible in a number of ways.

Use earthquakes to create mountain ranges.

Use meteors to create lakes.

Use meteors and hurricanes to increase rainfall.

Use earthquakes, volcanos and meteors to achieve the highest dust level you can.

Using only events (not the ALTITUDE tool), try to recreate the continents on Earth today. (Hint: you'll want to pause the simulation or at least turn the core heat all the way down to stop or slow continental drift.)

Play Bumper-continents. Get two or three friends, each build a small continent, and take turns setting off earthquakes to propel the continents into each other.

EVOLUTION TIME SCALE

The Evolution Time Scale comes after the Geologic Time Scale. It begins with the appearance of multicellular organisms and ends with the development of intelligence.

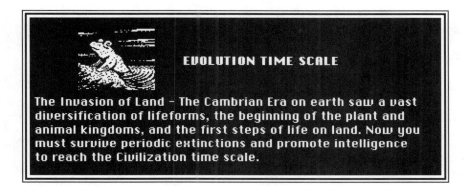

EVOLUTION TIME SCALE

The Invasion of Land – The Cambrian Era on earth saw a vast diversification of lifeforms, the beginning of the plant and animal kingdoms, and the first steps of life on land. Now you must survive periodic extinctions and promote intelligence to reach the Civilization time scale.

Things change a little faster in this Time Scale than in the Geologic, so the Time/ Simulation cycle has been lowered to 500,000 years.

Your available energy builds up at 1 E.U. per Time/Simulation cycle.

This Time Scale relates to the period of time on the real Earth from 570 to .01 million years ago.

The factors simulated in this Time Scale, in order of their influence, are: life, biomes, climate, atmospheric composition and continental drift.

The goal of this Time Scale is to manipulate the simulation factors and evolve intelligence, at which time you will be advanced to the Civilization Time Scale.

Your planet only has 10 billion years to live. If you want to complete all the Time Scales before the end of your planet, you should try to reach the next Time Scale when your planet is between five and six billion years old. Don't advance too soon, or there will not be enough fossil fuels for later civilizations.

SUMMARY—EVOLUTION TIME SCALE

Time/Simulation cycle   500,000 years
Energy increase/cycle   1 E.U.
Time on real Earth   570 to .01 billion years ago
Factors simulated   Life
                           Biomes
                           Climate
                           Atmospheric composition
                           Continental drift
Advancement conditions   Development of intelligence
Optimum advancement age   Between 5 and 6 billion years

THINGS TO DO:

Choose and help a particular class of life to develop intelligence.

Prevent particular species from developing intelligence.

Manipulate the evolutionary path.

Try to get Carniferns to reach intelligence without using the Monolith.

Try to get the highest biomass rating you can.

Try to maintain a valley or island of dinosaurs in the midst of a civilized world.

Play with the atmosphere and see what happens.

Raise the terrain all over the planet, and see what happens.

See how much and how little of your planet you can have as land without major repercussions to life.

The Civilization Time Scale comes after the Evolution time scale. It begins with the appearance of intelligent organisms and ends with the Industrial Revolution.

CIVILIZATION TIME SCALE

CIVILIZATION TIME SCALE

The evolution of intelligent life has brought you to the Civilization time scale. GAIA begins to achieve consciousness. Now you must spread your civilization across the planet and advance technology. The dawn of the industrial revolution will bring you into the Technology time scale.

Things change fast in this Time Scale, so the Time/Simulation cycle has been lowered to 10 years.

Your available energy builds up at different rates, depending on your highest available technology level:
2 E.U. per Time/Simulation cycle in the Stone Age,
3 E.U. per Time/Simulation cycle in the Bronze Age, and
4 E.U. per Time/Simulation cycle in the Iron Age.

This Time Scale relates to the period of time on the real Earth from 10,000 to 100 years ago.

The factors simulated in this Time Scale, in order of their influence, are: civilization, life, biomes, climate, and atmospheric composition.

The goal of this Time Scale is to manipulate the simulation factors and evolve higher levels of technology, at which time you will be advanced to the Technology Time Scale.

Your planet only has 10 billion years to live. If you want to complete all the Time Scales before the end of your planet, you should try to reach the next Time Scale before your planet is 9.5 billion years old.

SUMMARY—CIVILIZATION TIME SCALE

Time/Simulation cycle	10 years
Energy increase/cycle	2 E.U.—Stone Age
Energy increase/cycle	3 E.U.—Bronze Age
Energy increase/cycle	4 E.U.—Iron Age
Time on real Earth	10,000 to 100 years ago
Factors simulated	Civilization
	Life
	Biomes
	Climate
	Atmospheric composition
Advancement conditions	Development of higher technology
Optimum advancement age	Less than 9.5 billion years

THINGS TO DO:

Cause or prevent wars.

Eliminate unwanted technologies.

Promote or eliminate various energy sources.

Mold the sentient species to your liking through the CIVILIZATION MODEL CONTROL PANEL.

Improve the quality of life for your sentient species.

Set up equivalent civilizations on different continents, and let them race to the Technology age.

Vary the altitude, biomes, etc. for the two civilizations, and see what helps and hinders.

Try to control pollution.

The Technology Time Scale comes after the Civilization Time Scale. It begins with the appearance of high levels of technology, and ends when technology evolves to the level when your planet can reproduce itself through interstellar "genetic" seeding—the ability to colonize other planets.

TECHNOLOGY TIME SCALE

TECHNOLOGY TIME SCALE

The industrial revolution has occurred! Civilization grows rapidly now as breakthroughs are made in energy production, medicine and agriculture. But beware, civilization is also beginning to have a significant impact on the planet.

When you complete this Time Scale, and achieve interstellar migration, all civilization leaves the planet. The planet is then turned into a wildlife reserve, and returns to the Evolution Time Scale.

Things change very fast in this Time Scale, so the Time/Simulation cycle has been lowered to one year.

Your available energy builds up at different rates, depending on your highest available technology level:
5 E.U. per Time/Simulation cycle in the Industrial Age,
6 E.U. per Time/Simulation cycle in the Atomic Age,
7 E.U. per Time/Simulation cycle in the Information Age, and
8 E.U. per Time/Simulation cycle in the Nanotech Age.

This Time Scale relates to the period of time on the real Earth from 100 years ago to the future.

The factors simulated in this Time Scale, in order of their influence, are: civilization, life, biomes, sentient expansion, climate, and atmospheric composition.

The goal of this Time Scale is to manipulate the simulation factors and evolve a level of technology high enough to colonize other planets.

Your planet only has 10 billion years to live. You should try to complete this Time Scale before the end of your planet.

SUMMARY—TECHNOLOGY TIME SCALE

Time/Simulation cycle	1 year
Energy increase/cycle	5 E.U.—Industrial Age
Energy increase/cycle	6 E.U.—Atomic Age
Energy increase/cycle	7 E.U.—Information Age
Energy increase/cycle	8 E.U.—Nanotech Age
Time on real Earth	100 years ago to the future
Factors simulated	Civilization
	Life
	Biomes
	Climate
	Atmospheric composition
Advancement conditions	Development of high enough technology to colonize other planets.
Optimum advancement age	Less than 10 billion years old (before the planet dies)

THINGS TO DO:

Prevent the sentient creatures from destroying themselves.

Cause or prevent wars.

Eliminate unwanted technologies.

Return the planet to ignorant bliss.

Move cities of different technologies close to each other, and see what happens.

Control pollution.

Test the greenhouse effect.

SCENARIOS

There are six scenario planets included with SimEarth, plus the Daisyworld Scenario. They can all be played in easy, medium, hard, and experimental modes.

Each scenario has a task for you to accomplish, but feel free to just play with these worlds.

Scenarios are chosen and started in the NEW PLANET WINDOW.

AQUARIUM

Aquarium is a world that will never develop sentient life. Sentience can only be reached in SimEarth by land animals. We hope we're not offending any intelligent, purely aquatic aliens anywhere in the universe, but as far as we can tell, civilization requires the use of fire and the burning of fossil fuels to develop.

Intelligence in SimEarth requires land because of the need of fire, tools, and forges. Water creatures can reach intelligence, but need access to land for tool-making.

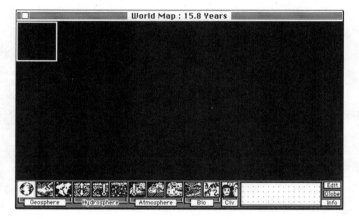

The problem: No continents

Time Scale: Evolution

Your mission: Create continents on this planet so civilization can evolve.

The methods: The easy way is to use the SET ALTITUDE tool. A more creative approach is to use events. The most subtle method is by manipulating the MODEL CONTROL PANELS.

Hints: Make sure you keep plenty of shelves (shallow water) in your oceans. Most marine life lives near the surface.

Notes: Aquarium is a good starting place for people who like to design their own continents.

STAG NATION

The civilization on this world is trapped in the Stone Age. The sentient mammals are all stuck on a small island. They have no room to expand, and are unable to develop or expend energy for a technological jump.

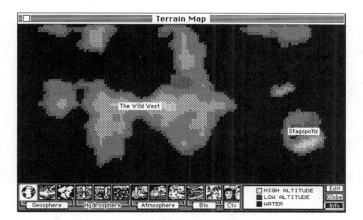

The problem: Population stuck in the Stone Age.

Time Scale: Civilization

Your mission: Aid the population in a migration to larger land masses, and increase their level of science.

The methods: The advancement in science will require manipulation of the CIVILIZATION MODEL CONTROL PANEL. The migration can be performed in a number of ways: pick them up and move them to a larger landmass with the MOVING tool; build a land bridge for them to cross with the SET ALTITUDE tool; or use events.

Hints : If you use events to make a land bridge, be careful not to wipe out your sentient population by accident.

Notes: If you don't like intelligent Mammals, you can destroy the island where they live, and try to nurture another class of life to sentience.

EARTH: THE CAMBRIAN ERA

This scenario takes place on Earth 550 million years ago at the beginning of the Cambrian era. Life on Earth at that time was undergoing an explosion of diversification. Plants started moving onto the land, followed by insects and other animals.

In this scenario, the drift of the continents will follow the drift of Earth's continents. It starts with the supercontinent called Pangaea, which then splits apart into the ancient continents of Gondwanaland and Laurasia.

Eventually, you will recognize the continents as we see them today. The pre-programmed drift will continue into the future following scientific predictions for about 200 million years. After that, the simulation takes over and controls the drift.

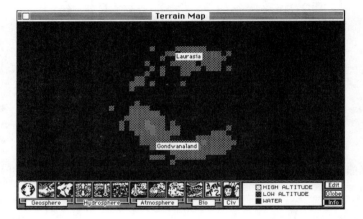

The problem: Living in the past

Time Scale: Evolution

Your mission: Help evolution develop intelligent life while seeing an instant replay of our planet's continental drift.

The methods: On this one, you can just sit back and watch, or get involved in every planetary process. The continents will drift whether or not any life is around to see where they go.

Hints: Beyond 200 million years in the future, the drift will diverge from scientific predictions, and will be at the whim of our simulation code.

To see a real instant replay of the continental drift, click and hold on the INFO BOX and slowly drag the mouse back and forth.

Any changes you make to the continents by using events will disappear. The continental drift will follow its pre-programmed path no matter what you do.

Notes: Try to develop intelligence/civilization in your sentient species just as the continents reach the stage of modern Earth. See if you can create an earth with intelligent dinosaurs.

EARTH: MODERN DAY

This scenario takes place on the Earth of today. We live in a world with pollution, war, famine, greenhouse warming, energy shortages, and the possibility of nuclear winter.

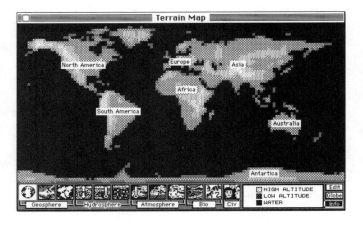

The problems: Too many to list here. Read your newspaper.

Time Scale: Technology

Your mission: Solve all the world's problems and lead us into a future of peace, abundant food, clean air, and plentiful energy.

The methods: If I knew how to solve all these problems, I'd be running the U.N. instead of making computer games.

Hints: The best way to prevent war in SimEarth is to allocate energy to philosophy in the CIVILIZATION MODEL CONTROL PANEL. Increasing allocation to Agriculture will increase the food supply. Allocating to Art/Media improves the quality of life. Wars and plague have a greater impact in this scenario than they do in the real world.

Notes: This scenario can be difficult, but still more fun than the real thing. If you click and hold on the Terrain Map Icon in the MAP WINDOW, you will see the names of the continents displayed. If you click and hold on the Drift icon in the MAP WINDOW you will see the names of the major tectonic plates displayed.

MARS

For this scenario, you are a citizen in a nanotech level society. Your home planet is overcrowded, and the population is increasing.

You show up for work, and find a memo from the boss that informs you that you've been put in charge of a new project. The promotion involves a small raise, but you'll have to move—to Mars. Your new job is to turn Mars into a planet capable of supporting human life. If you fail to complete this project within 500 years you'll be fired.

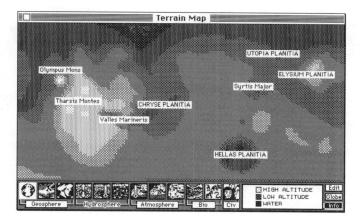

The problem: No water, almost no atmospheric pressure, no oxygen, no plants, no animals, no nothing—except rock. The average temperature is -53 degrees C.

Time Scale: Technology

Your mission: Terraform Mars and make it a place fit for human occupation, and colonize the planet.

The methods: The MODEL CONTROL PANELS (except for the CIVILIZATION MODEL CONTROL PANEL) have been disabled to make this a challenge. You'll need the TERRAFORMERS available through the PLACE LIFE tool. Gaian regulation has been disabled—no life will spontaneously generate. The REPORT WINDOW gives you special feedback on your terraforming progress.

Hints: Start off with a few ice meteors to create oceans. Then start producing CO_2 and other greenhouse gases to build up atmospheric pressure and begin planetary warming. Use the CO_2 generator or better yet, plant some single-celled life in the oceans—they are more efficient than terraformers at building an atmosphere.

Notes: Click and hold on the TERRAIN MAP icon in the MAP WINDOW to see a display of Martian landmarks. Landmark names shown in all capital letters designate large regions, other names designate smaller regions or individual spots.

VENUS

Venus is SimEarth's ultimate challenge in terraforming. While Mars is far too cold, Venus is far too hot for life: its average temperature is 477 degrees C.

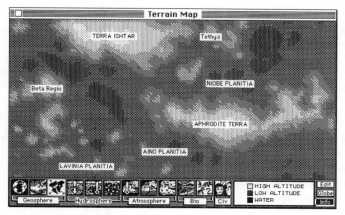

The problem: Too hot for life

Time Scale: Technology

Your mission: Cool this planet down, and make it a fit place for Earth life-forms.

The methods: The MODEL CONTROL PANELS (except for the CIVILIZATION MODEL CONTROL PANEL) have been disabled. You'll need the TERRAFORMERS available through the PLACE LIFE tool. Gaian regulation has been disabled—no life will spontaneously generate. The REPORT WINDOW gives you special feedback on your terraforming progress.

Hints: The first thing you have to do is cool the planet down. Ice meteors won't help—but go ahead and try them if you want. It's so hot that ice meteors melt and boil off into water vapor. Since water vapor is a greenhouse gas, it just makes things hotter.

To cool things down, you've got to reduce the greenhouse effect. The Oxygenator takes CO_2 (a greenhouse gas) out of the atmosphere. As soon as it cools enough, start placing biomes on Venus, which will also lower the CO_2 in the air. When placing biomes, remember that the higher the elevation, the cooler the temperature.

Notes: Click and hold on the TERRAIN MAP icon in the MAP WINDOW to see a display of Venusian landmarks. Landmark names shown in all capital letters designate large regions, other names designate smaller regions.

DAISYWORLD

Unlike the other scenario planets, the terrain of Daisyworld is randomly generated each time you load it.

According to the Gaia theory, life and the environment together constitute a system that self-regulates climate and atmospheric composition.

This scenario is based on the original Daisyworld program James Lovelock developed as a test of the Gaia theory.

During the past 3.6 billion years, the output of heat from the Sun has increased by 25%, but the Earth's average temperature has remained almost unchanged during the same time period.

According to theory, Gaia has controlled the temperature to keep Earth cool enough for life. Daisyworld tests Gaia's ability to regulate temperature.

In Daisyworld, as in all SimEarth planets and scenarios (and real life), the Sun's heat output is slowly but constantly increasing. If Gaian regulation works, the average temperature on the planet should remain fairly constant in spite of the increasing solar radiation.

The biomes have been changed to eight shades of Daisies. The different shades, ranging from white to black, reflect different amounts of light and heat that regulate the planet's temperature.

Daisies are available for planting in the PLANT BIOME tool. The ratio of the various shades of Daisies can be tracked in the BIOME RATIO GRAPH.

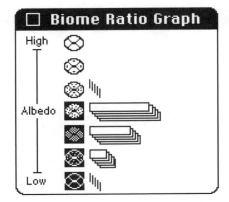

The problem: The heat from the Sun is steadily increasing. If it isn't somehow regulated, the oceans will boil off and all life on this planet will die.

Time Scale: N/A

Your mission: Test Gaia's ability to regulate temperature, and fill the world with Daisies.

The methods: Keep an eye on the Temperature Map and the Air Temperature graph in the HISTORY WINDOW to observe the regulation cycles.

The REPORT WINDOW gives you special feedback on your Daisy-raising progress.

Hints and cautions: Place life on the planet to eat the Daisies. See how this complication affects regulation.

Notes: There will eventually be a breakdown point where the heat from the Sun is too great for Gaia to regulate. Adding or subtracting land areas where Daisies can live will move this breakdown point forward or backwards.

Also note the change in the Daisies' color as the landmass increases and decreases.

Try testing the stability of the system by killing off many of the Daisies. How many can be killed before the system collapses? How much of the planet's surface must be covered by Daisies for regulation to occur?

HOW DAISYWORLD WORKS

Daisyworld is a planet like Earth, but with few clouds and a constant low concentration of greenhouse gases. The output from the planet's sun is constantly increasing.

The planet's temperature is a balance between the heat received from the sun and the heat loss by radiation from the planet to space. The albedo—the reflectiveness—of the planet determines the temperature.

The planet is well-seeded with Daisies, whose growth rate is a function of temperature. There are two colors of Daisies: Black and White, which only grow between 5 and 40 degrees C, and grow best at 22.5 degrees C. Assume plenty of water and nutrients for the plants.

Taking into account only the heat from the sun and the albedo of the planet, we get the results in the following graphs.

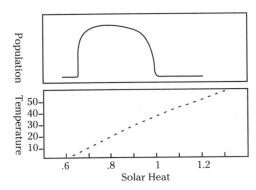

The bottom graph shows the increasing solar heat (dotted line). The temperature of the planet rises in direct proportion to the increase of solar heat. The top graph shows life on the planet (Daisies) during the same time.

When the temperature hits 5 degrees C the Daisies begin to grow. When the temperature hits 40 degrees C they all die.

Now we add the albedo (heat and light reflectiveness) of the Daisies to the system.

When the planet's temperature reaches 5 degrees C, Daisies begin to grow. During the first season, the Black Daisies will grow better since they will be warmer than the planet's surface (dark colors absorb heat). White Daisies won't grow very well, since they reflect heat and will be colder than the planet's surface.

At the end of the first season there will be many more Black Daisy seeds in the soil that will soon grow. As the Black Daisies spread, they will not only warm themselves, but the whole planet.

Eventually, because of the warming from both the Black Daisies and the Sun, the planet's temperature will rise to 22.5 degrees C. Since the Black Daisies are warmer than the planet, they are above their optimum living temperature, and their growth rate will slow.

Since the White Daisies are cooler than the planet, they will start to grow better as the temperature gets higher. When there are enough White Daisies, they will reflect enough heat to cool the planet.

The results are shown in the graphs on the next page.

The bottom graph still shows the same rise in solar heat (dotted line). It also shows the planetary temperatures (solid line) which have been affected by the presence of the Daisies.

The top graph shows the population of the two types of Daisies—when it's colder the Black Daisies grow better and as it warms up, the White ones grow better.

Eventually, the solar heat gets so great that the White Daisies cannot reflect enough heat to cool the planet.

The important thing to note here is that the life on the planet affected the climate of the planet in a way that is beneficial to life. It regulated the temperature, and nearly doubled the amount of time life could survive.

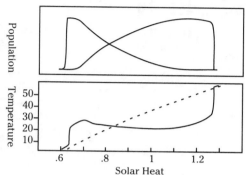

This is only a simple demonstration, and only deals with one life-form and one climactic feature, but it does demonstrates the two-way connection between life and environment.

INSIDE THE SIMULATION

EVENTS

Events are noteworthy occurrences on your planet. They will happen randomly, controlled by the simulation, and you can cause most of them to happen through the TRIGGER EVENTS TOOL in the EDIT WINDOW.

The cost in energy for triggering an event is 50 E.U.

There are 11 events in SimEarth, eight of which can be triggered manually:

    HURRICANE—A Hurricane is a tropical cyclone with winds of 74 m.p.h. or greater, usually accompanied by rain, thunder and lightning. Hurricanes can cause tidal waves.

They can wipe out cities and destroy a lot of life. In SimEarth, hurricanes are caused by warm oceans. The only way to defend against them is to keep your oceans cool.

You can use hurricanes to increase rainfall in specific areas on your planet.

    TIDAL WAVE—An unusually high sea wave that can be caused by earthquakes, high winds, hurricanes, volcanos and meteor impact.

Tidal waves can destroy coastal cities and land life. They generally travel from deeper water to shallower water.

Tidal waves are useful for eliminating unwanted coastal cities.

    METEOR—Meteors are huge hunks of rock from space that smash into the planet, causing much damage and creating craters on land and tidal waves in the sea.

Meteors that crash into the land will put dust into the air. Too much dust will block the sun and cause extinctions. Meteors that crash into water put water vapor into the air, increasing rainfall. Meteorites also affect magma flow.

Meteors are useful for adding water vapor to the atmosphere (increasing rainfall), creating lakes in large land masses, and destroying pesky life-forms.

    VOLCANO—A volcano is a vent in the planetary crust that lets a flow of molten rock to the surface. Volcanos raise the terrain elevation, creating mountains on land and islands in the sea. Volcanos in the ocean cause tidal waves. The severity of volcanos is less when the planet is young and the core is large.

Volcanos in SimEarth are huge upwellings that make recent real Earth events like Krakatoa look like pimples.

Volcanos put a lot of dust into the air, which can block the sun and cause extinctions. They also add a lot of carbon dioxide to the air, which is great for plants, but above a certain point, bad for animals.

Volcanos are useful for creating islands and mountains, and for doing general damage to life-forms.

    ATOMIC TEST—Atomic tests are the firings of atomic bombs. They occur "naturally" in wars between groups of your sentient species.

Atomic tests do much damage, spread radiation, and put a lot of dust into the atmosphere. Too many atomic tests can cause a nuclear winter, which causes mass extinctions.

    Areas that are contaminated by radiation are marked with this symbol.

Atomic tests are useful as a destructive tool, and for testing the effects of nuclear winter.

    FIRE—Fires occur when the oxygen content of your atmosphere is too high. To protect against fires, keep your oxygen levels down.

Fires are useful for regulating the oxygen in your atmosphere, and causing general destruction.

    EARTHQUAKE—A major shake-up of an area of the planet. When you point to the Trigger Earthquake option a sub-submenu will appear, allowing you to select the direction of energy expended by the earthquake. This will let you affect continental drift. Earthquakes under water will cause tidal waves.

When earthquakes appear naturally in SimEarth, they occur at plate boundaries (places where two land masses meet). To avoid damage from earthquakes, don't place cities near plate boundaries. To find these boundaries, look at the MAGMA display in the EDIT WINDOW. Wherever arrows that point in different directions are next to each other is a plate boundary.

In SimEarth, earthquakes are very useful events. You can use them to affect the movement of land masses, and change the magma flow. Forcing two land masses into movement toward each other is a fun way to create a mountain range.

To easily see the effect your earthquake has on the planet, turn on the MAGMA layer in the EDIT WINDOW before you trigger it, and watch the direction of the magma flow arrows change.

This is actually the opposite of what happens in the real world. We have reversed cause and effect. In reality, earthquakes are caused by the movement of the plate boundaries, and don't cause or change magma flow. It's not accurate, but it's a great tool for making mountain ranges.

PLAGUE—Plagues are very dangerous diseases that can wipe out entire cities, and will spread to nearby cities. They happen more often in low-technology areas, but once they happen there, they can spread to nearby high-technology areas.

To prevent plagues, you must invest in Medicine in the CIVILIZATION MODEL CONTROL PANEL.

Plagues aren't useful for anything but destruction.

 WAR—Wars cannot be triggered by the TRIGGER EVENTS icon. War in SimEarth represents battles between cities, as well as rebellions and revolutions within cities.

Wars are often caused by competition for resources such as fossil and atomic fuel. This is a self-regulating process: Cities grow too big, too close, and too fast for the local fuel supply; they go to war over the fuel; they kill enough of each other off so they can all live happily on the existing fuel; then they declare peace.

Sometimes wars just happen—SimEarthlings can be as stupid as Earthlings.

World wars occur in higher technology levels, and consist of lots of battles going on all over the planet.

The only way to prevent wars, or reduce the number and severity of wars, is by allocating energy to Philosophy in the CIVILIZATION MODEL CONTROL PANEL.

 POLLUTION—Pollution events are warnings that the pollution in an area of your planet has reached levels that are dangerous to life.

They are primarily caused by industrial waste and pollutants, and can only be prevented and controlled by investing in non-polluting energy sources.

Pollution events cannot be triggered by the TRIGGER EVENTS tool, but if you want one, invest heavily in fossil fuels.

    EXODUS—When the sentient SimEarthlings reach a high enough level of development, they leave the planet to colonize other worlds. The planet is then "retired" to the status of a wildlife preserve to be visited and cherished.

At this point, the planet returns to the Evolution Time Scale, and the race to sentience begins again.

THE EXODUS

With the advent of nano-technology, all levels of society gain access to scientific benefits. The stars are now only a short step away. Whole cities are fitted with engines to launch them skyward, and the Exodus begins. The home world becomes a nature preserve, allowing evolution to continue.

The EXODUS event is the closest thing in SimEarth to a "win condition."

The Geosphere in SimEarth simulates planet formation, planetary cooling, continental drift, volcanic activity and erosion. For an explanation of geology and atmosphere of the real Earth, take a look at the Introduction to Earth Science section.

GEOSPHERE

PLANET FORMATION

SimEarth simulates a planet just after interstellar dust has condensed into a lump of dirt. It is tightly packed, with a molten core. The surface is solid, but the surface temperature is still very hot. The atmosphere is mostly steam.

The flowing currents in the molten core cause parts of the solid surface of the planet to start moving around, crashing into each other. This crashing results in the creation of huge mountains and deep ditches.

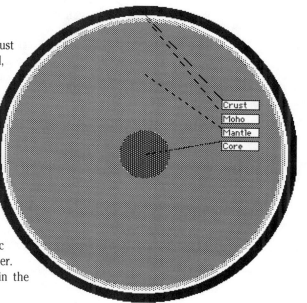

PLANETARY COOLING

With time, the core of the planet solidifies to a plastic consistency, and gets larger as the planet gets older. The rate at which the core forms can be set in the GEOSPHERE MODEL CONTROL PANEL.

The larger the core, the smaller the magma layer. The smaller the magma layer, the slower the magma currents, and the slower the continental drift.

CONTINENTAL DRIFT

Continental drift is the movement of the solid crust of the planet on the liquid magma inside the planet. The faster and stronger the magma currents, the faster the drift. Continental drift is also affected by core heat. The rate of continental drift can be set in the GEOSPHERE MODEL CONTROL PANEL.

CORE HEAT

Core heat is the temperature of the planet's core. The higher the core heat, the larger and more severe the volcanos are. Also, the hotter the core, the more the direction of magma flow will change. Core heat can be adjusted in the GEOSPHERE MODEL CONTROL PANEL.

FORMATION OF THE OCEANS

The planet eventually cools enough for the steam in the atmosphere to condense and form oceans. Once oceans are formed, your planet is ready for life.

VOLCANIC ACTIVITY

Volcanos are vents in the surface of the planet that allow magma to flow to the surface. The volcanos in SimEarth are huge explosive events that make recent volcanic activities like Krakatoa look like pimples. When volcanos occur in water, they create islands. When they occur on land, they create great mountains. The frequency and violence of volcanos is directly affected by core heat.

You can also control the frequency and violence of volcanos with the GEOSPHERE MODEL CONTROL PANEL.

EROSION

Erosion is the "smoothing" of the terrain by wind and water. Younger planets will have higher, more jagged mountains than older planets that have suffered the effects of erosion longer. Erosion also creates large continental shelves. The rate of erosion can be set in the GEOSPHERE MODEL CONTROL PANEL.

Erosion increases the CO_2 level in the atmosphere.

The atmosphere in SimEarth consists of four gases—Nitrogen (N_2), Oxygen (O_2), Carbon Dioxide (CO_2) and Methane (CH_4)—plus water vapor (H_2O) and dust particles.

NITROGEN

Nitrogen is released by the soil through geochemical reactions with the air, and is absorbed into the soil by microbes. It is also released into the atmosphere by volcanos. It is the most common gas in the atmosphere.

OXYGEN

Oxygen is released into the atmosphere by plants and microbes during photosynthesis. It is consumed by animals and fires. Too little oxygen in the atmosphere (<15%) and animal life can't survive. Too much oxygen (>25%) and fires will break out all over the planet. Fires act as an oxygen regulator.

CARBON DIOXIDE

Carbon dioxide is released into the atmosphere by geochemical reactions and erosion, and is absorbed by plants and microbes. Too little carbon dioxide (<.1%) and plants can't survive. Carbon dioxide is a greenhouse gas, and will contribute to global warming due to the greenhouse effect. If your CO_2 level exceeds 1% you will have greenhouse warming.

METHANE

Methane is released into the atmosphere by bacteria (prokaryotes). It is a greenhouse gas, and will contribute to global warming through the greenhouse effect.

WATER VAPOR

Water vapor evaporates from warm oceans and lakes, and returns to the land and seas through rainfall. Water vapor in the atmosphere is increased by hurricanes and meteors hitting the oceans. Water vapor is a greenhouse gas.

DUST PARTICLES

Dust is released into the air by volcanic activity, fires, nuclear explosions, and meteor strikes. Too much dust in the atmosphere causes solar blockage, planetary cooling, and mass extinctions.

ATMOSPHERIC PRESSURE

Atmospheric pressure is a measure of how much atmosphere, by weight, is around the planet. The air pressure of the real Earth is 1.0 atmospheres. A higher atmospheric pressure allows a planet to better retain heat.

TRACKING THE ATMOSPHERE

You can keep track of your atmospheric composition by watching the ATMOSPHERIC COMPOSITION GRAPH.

The climate of SimEarth is much simpler than on the real Earth. When modeling climate, SimEarth primarily takes into account air currents, air temperature, and rainfall.

CLIMATE

Air currents, air temperature, and rainfall are influenced by sea temperature, ocean currents, solar input, cloud formation, cloud albedo, surface albedo, greenhouse effect, air-sea thermal transfer, and atmospheric pressure.

In addition, ice caps indirectly affect climate through their ability to cool the planet. Cold oceans are necessary for ice caps to form.

In SimEarth, as on the real Earth, the heat from the Sun is slowly increasing.

AIR CURRENTS
The planetary winds.

AIR TEMPERATURE
The average annual air temperature. The heat displayed here comes primarily from the sun, and secondarily from warm ocean areas.

RAINFALL
The amount of rainfall on the planet. It includes all types of precipitation.

SEA TEMPERATURE
The average annual ocean temperature. In most cases this will correspond closely with the air temperature, but it will change much more slowly.

OCEAN CURRENTS
The surface currents of the oceans.

SOLAR INPUT
The incoming solar radiation, also called *Insolation*. This is the amount of energy that reaches the planet from the sun.

CLOUD FORMATION
The amount of clouds formed from a given amount of evaporation.

CLOUD ALBEDO
The reflectivity of the clouds, which controls the amount of sunlight (heat) that passes through them to the planet.

SURFACE ALBEDO
The reflectivity of surface biomes, and therefore the amount of sunlight (heat) which is blocked by them.

GREENHOUSE EFFECT
The planet-warming greenhouse effect. The greenhouse effect is caused by certain gases that block outgoing infrared radiation. This keeps more of the Sun's heat in the atmosphere, which warms the whole planet. In SimEarth, the greenhouse gases are water vapor (H_2O), methane (CH_4), and carbon dioxide (CO_2).

AIR-SEA THERMAL TRANSFER
The rate at which the air and ocean can exchange heat.

ATMOSPHERIC PRESSURE
A measure of how much atmosphere, by weight, is around the planet. The air pressure of the real Earth is 1.0 atmospheres. A higher atmospheric pressure allows a planet to better retain heat.

AFFECTING CLIMATE
You can affect the way SimEarth models climate by changing the settings on the ATMOSPHERE MODEL CONTROL PANEL.

LIFE AND EVOLUTION

As far as the model in SimEarth is concerned, life is any plant or animal on your planet.

The number and variety of plants, animals, niches and biomes included in SimEarth has been limited to enable the model to run on a home computer, but there are enough to demonstrate the principles involved with planet management.

ORIGINS OF LIFE IN SIMEARTH

In SimEarth, the only necessary factor for life to form is the presence of some deep sea (greater than 2500 meters deep) or ocean (between 1000 and 2500 meters deep). We assume the presence of all necessary chemicals and elements.

Ocean will form as soon as the planet cools, and if there is some deep ocean, life will form.

LIFE HAS FORMED

In the primordial soup the replicator is born. A molecule with the unique property of self-replication, the replicator begins making copies of itself. The thread of life begins.

The formation of life on the real Earth is much more complicated, and still very controversial.

LIFE IN SIMEARTH

Life in SimEarth is much simpler and less varied than on the real Earth. SimEarth has 15 classes of life, each with 16 species. The real Earth has millions of species.

SimEarth has seven biomes, the real Earth has many more.

EVOLUTION IN SIMEARTH

Evolution in SimEarth depends on many factors. For sea life to evolve, there must be shallow shelves. For land life, there must be the proper atmosphere, with enough carbon dioxide, oxygen, and air pressure. The air and water temperatures must be within livable limits. And there must be enough of the proper biome for the life to evolve in.

Life advances from simple to more complex forms, and, hopefully, to intelligence.

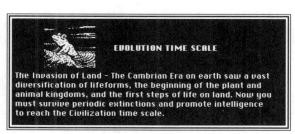

EVOLUTION TIME SCALE

The Invasion of Land - The Cambrian Era on earth saw a vast diversification of lifeforms, the beginning of the plant and animal kingdoms, and the first steps of life on land. Now you must survive periodic extinctions and promote intelligence to reach the Civilization time scale.

Evolutionary advancement also depends on population size. The more of a life-form you have on your planet, the more likely it is to advance to another level.

There are two sizes of steps SimEarthlings can take in their progress towards sentience: ADVANCEMENT and MUTATION.

ADVANCEMENT is a small step. It is a step up to a more complex species, but stays within the same class of life. The ADVANCEMENT RATE can be set in the BIOSPHERE MODEL CONTROL PANEL.

MUTATION RATE is a big step. It is a jump to a new class of life.

COMPETITION

There is competition within the evolutionary process. If two life-forms land on the same spot, the more advanced one will kill the other. The rating of which life-form is more advanced than another involves, among other smaller factors, the class, the species, and the IQ of each life-form. Some of these factors change over time and vary with the planet, so there can be no win/lose chart of life-form rankings.

Also, if and when a new, higher class of life mutates, it will take precedence over all lower forms.

BIOMES IN SIMEARTH

There are seven available biomes in SimEarth, plus ROCK, which represents a lack of a biome in a location. To survive and spread, biomes require carbon dioxide and rainfall.

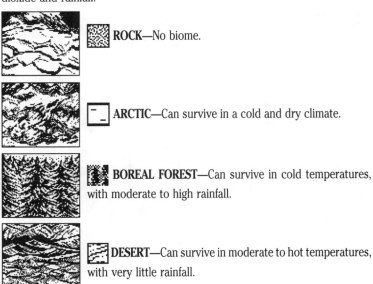

ROCK—No biome.

ARCTIC—Can survive in a cold and dry climate.

BOREAL FOREST—Can survive in cold temperatures, with moderate to high rainfall.

DESERT—Can survive in moderate to hot temperatures, with very little rainfall.

TEMPERATE GRASSLANDS—Can survive in areas with moderate temperatures and rainfall.

 FOREST—Can survive with moderate temperatures and high rainfall.

 JUNGLE—Can survive with high temperatures and rainfall.

 SWAMP—Can survive with high temperatures and moderate rainfall.

BIOME PREFERENCE CHART

	DRY (<30 cm/yr)	**MODERATE** (30–90 cm/yr)	**WET** (>90 cm/yr)
COLD (<0° C)	Arctic	Boreal Forest	Boreal Forest
MODERATE (0–25° C)	Desert	Temp. Grasslands	Forest
HOT (>25° C)	Desert	Swamp	Jungle

Biome preferences are also influenced by altitude and the amount of CO_2 in the atmosphere.

LIFE-FORMS IN SIMEARTH

There are 15 classes of life represented in SimEarth; eight on land, seven in the sea. Only 14 of these are available in the PLACE LIFE tool. The 15th, the Carniferns—mobile, carnivorous plants that can evolve sapience—will sometimes appear through evolution.

Each class consists of 16 species. There are a total of 240 species in SimEarth. If a class of life reaches the 16th species, it becomes sentient. You will never see the 16th species of many of the classes unless you can help that class develop intelligence.

Below is an explanation of each class of life, with a graphic of all 16 species for that class of life. The possible evolutionary advancements and mutations are also shown. Advancement is in steps from left to right through all the species of that class. Mutation is a jump to a new class.

For each class of life below is a chart of its possible evolutionary paths. The progression of advancement within the same class, from simplest to most advanced (intelligent) is shown from left to right. Possible mutations to higher classes of life are shown as steps up.

Only certain species within a class of life can mutate. There are many evolutionary dead-ends.

SEA LIFE CLASSES

 PROKARYOTE—Simple single-celled life that has no distinct nucleus, including bacteria and blue-green algae. Prokaryotes release methane into the atmosphere. In SimEarth, Prokaryotes are all treated as anaerobic, methane-consuming organisms, which is an extreme simplification.

The eight most advanced Prokaryote species can possibly mutate to Eukaryotes.

Eukaryote

 EUKARYOTE—Single-celled life with a nucleus; includes all single-celled life except prokaryotes. In SimEarth, all Eukaryotes are treated as aerobic, photosynthesizing organisms, which is an extreme simplification.

Eukaryotes evolve from Prokaryotes. The four most evolved species of Eukaryote can mutate into Radiates.

Radiate

RADIATE—Simple, radially symmetrical multicellular life with definite tissue layers (three at most), but no distinct internal organs, head, or central nervous system. Includes jellyfish and sea anemones.

Radiates evolve from Eukaryotes. The first eight species of Radiate can mutate into Arthropods. The next four species can mutate into Trichordates.

Arthropod   Trichordate

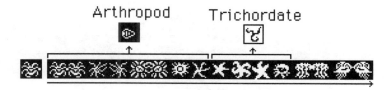

 ARTHROPOD—Animals with jointed legs and a hard outer skeleton, including crabs, lobsters, and crayfish. (Spiders, scorpions, centipedes, millipedes, and insects are also arthropods, but they live on land.)

Arthropods evolve from Radiates. The first four species of Arthropod can mutate into Mollusks, the next eight can mutate into Insects.

Mollusk   Insect

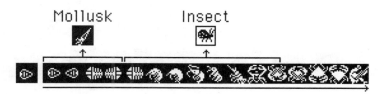

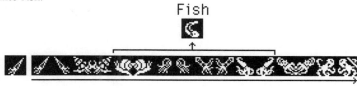 **MOLLUSK**—Fairly complex animals, most of which possess shells, including snails, clams, oysters, scallops, octopi, and squid.

Mollusks evolve from Arthropods. The middle eight species of Mollusks can mutate into Fish.

Fish

FISH—Very advanced and complex sea life with an internal bony skeleton.

Fish evolve from Mollusks. The first eight species of Fish can mutate into Amphibians, the next four species can mutate into Trichordates.

Amphibian   Trichordate

CETACEAN—Marine mammals with a highly developed nervous system, including whales, dolphins, and porpoises. Cetaceans can survive in Jungle biomes, as shown in the chart of Life Classes and Preferred Biomes. They actually live in the Jungle's rivers and tributaries that are too small to show in the EDIT WINDOW.

Cetaceans evolve from Mammals. The last four species of Cetacean can mutate back into Mammals.

Mammal

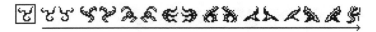

LAND LIFE CLASSES

TRICHORDATE—Trichordates were a class of animal with three-chord spines. They lived and died out long ago on real Earth. We felt sorry for them, and are giving them a chance for survival in SimEarth.

Trichordates evolve from Radiates and/or Fish. They cannot mutate into anything else.

INSECT—The most numerous type of life on Earth, they have six legs and three body sections.

Insects evolve from Arthropods. Insects don't evolve into anything else, but, as shown in the chart, there is a co-evolution situation with Carniferns. The Carniferns don't actually evolve from Insects: they evolve from plants because of the presence of Insects.

AMPHIBIAN—Cold-blooded vertebrates somewhere between fish and reptiles, including frogs, toads, and newts.

Amphibians evolve from Fish. The first eight species of Amphibians can mutate into Reptiles.

REPTILE—Cold-blooded vertebrates, including alligators, crocodiles, lizards, snakes, and turtles.

Reptiles evolve from Amphibians. The first eight species of Reptile can mutate into Dinosaurs. The next four species can mutate into Mammals.

 DINOSAUR—Very big reptiles that long ago died out on real Earth. SimEarth gives them a new lease on life.

Dinosaurs evolve from Reptiles. The first four species of Dinosaurs can mutate into Avians. The next four species can mutate into Mammals.

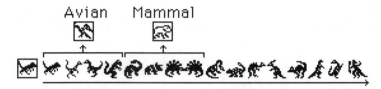

 AVIAN—(A fancy word for bird.) Warm-blooded vertebrates with bodies more or less completely covered by feathers, with wings for forelimbs.

Avians evolve from Dinosaurs. Avians cannot mutate into anything else.

MAMMAL—The highest form of vertebrate, including man, apes, rodents, dogs, cats, etc. Mammals nourish their young with milk secreted from mammary glands, and have skin more or less covered with hair.

Mammals evolve from Cetaceans, Reptiles, and/or Dinosaurs. The middle eight species of Mammals can evolve into Cetaceans.

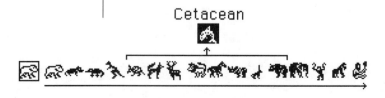

CARNIFERNS—Carniferns will evolve, but are not available to manually place with the PLACE LIFE tool. They are mobile, carnivorous plants that for simulation purposes are treated like animals. They are just above insects in evolutionary complexity, and evolved from plants taking advantage of insects as a food source. They can achieve intelligence, but it is rare.

Carniferns co-evolve with Insects. They actually evolve from plants, but their existence depends of the existence of Insects.

CHART OF LIFE CLASSES AND PREFERRED BIOMES

Legend:
- **X** Life class cannot exist here.
- **(barely)** Can exist here, but barely.
- **(fair)** Can exist here fairly well.
- **(paradise)** Paradise.

Life Class	Shelf	Ocean	Deep Sea	Rock	Arctic	Boreal	Desert	Grass	Forest	Jungle	Swamp
Prokaryote	paradise	paradise	barely	X	X	X	X	X	X	X	X
Eukaryote	paradise	paradise	barely	X	X	X	X	X	X	X	X
Radiate	paradise	paradise	fair	X	X	X	X	X	X	barely	barely
Arthropod	paradise	paradise	X	X	X	X	X	X	X	barely	fair
Mollusk	paradise	paradise	X	X	X	X	X	X	X	fair	fair
Fish	paradise	paradise	fair	X	X	X	X	X	X	X	X
Cetacean	paradise	paradise	X	X	X	X	X	X	X	fair	X
Trichordate	barely	X	X	X	X	barely	barely	barely	barely	barely	fair
Insect	barely	X	X	X	X	fair	fair	fair	fair	fair	fair
Amphibian	barely	X	X	X	X	barely	X	fair	fair	barely	barely
Reptile	barely	X	X	X	X	fair	fair	fair	fair	fair	fair
Dinosaur	barely	X	X	X	X	fair	barely	barely	barely	fair	fair
Avian	barely	X	X	X	X	barely	barely	fair	barely	barely	barely
Mammal	barely	X	X	X	X	fair	fair	barely	fair	fair	fair
Carnifern	barely	X	X	X	X	X	barely	barely	barely	barely	barely

CIVILIZATION

CIVILIZATIONS IN SIMEARTH

There are seven levels of civilization represented in SimEarth, from the Stone Age of our past to the Nanotech Age of our future. For an in-depth look at these civilizations as they appeared on the real Earth, see the Introduction to Earth Science section of this manual.

Civilizations are represented by cities and travelling populations. Each city has three different population densities; the darker the city icon, the higher the population. Travelling populations represent expansion, communication and trade, and travel between cities.

The Nanotech age has four levels of density, and no travelling population. We assume they use transporters for trade and travel.

The advance of technology is a double-edged sword. Higher technology allows more efficient use of energy, shorter working weeks, and a higher quality of life. It also allows pollution, competition for fuel sources, wars, world wars, atomic wars, and other by-products of advanced civilization.

Below is a description of the civilizations in SimEarth with the graphics for the three (or four) levels of density and the travelling populations (if any), as they are displayed over land and over water.

STONE AGE—The Stone Age in SimEarth relates to civilizations on the real Earth thought to begin as far back as a million years ago, and lasting, in some places on the Earth, until today. It is characterized by the use of stone tools.

BRONZE AGE—The Bronze Age began with the regular use of metals for tools and weapons. The earliest established Bronze Age dates back to 3500 B.C. in the Middle East.

IRON AGE—The Iron Age began nearly 2000 years ago, and still exists in places today. It is characterized by the use of iron for tools and weapons.

 **INDUSTRIAL AGE**—The Industrial Age in SimEarth relates to the time from the Industrial Revolution of the mid-18th century to the beginning of the Atomic Age. It is characterized by the use advanced tools and powered machinery.

  **ATOMIC AGE**—The Atomic Age begins with the use of atomic energy. It is the present highest technology level on the real Earth.

  **INFORMATION AGE**—The Information Age in SimEarth is the next technological step after the Atomic Age. In this age, information is the most important tool.

 NANOTECH AGE—The ultimate level of technology in SimEarth is reached in the Nanotech Age. This is far enough in the future that we can only guess and dream about it. It will be characterized by a level of sophistication and technology that allows terraforming and colonizing other planets.

The Nanotech Age has four levels of density, and no travelling population. We assume they use transporters for trade and travel.

ALTERNATE INTELLIGENT SPECIES

SimEarth doesn't limit intelligent species to humans or even just mammals. Any class of life—other than Prokaryote and Eukaryote—can become intelligent.

Development of civilization in SimEarth requires land because of the need of fire, tools, and forges. Water creatures can be civilized, but need access to land for toolmaking.

In SimEarth, the most likely classes of life to evolve intelligence are: reptiles, dinosaurs, birds, and mammals.

The next most likely group are: cetaceans, insects, amphibians, and carniferns.

The least likely to evolve intelligence are: radiates, mollusks, arthropods and fish.

Aside from the above ranking, the evolution of intelligence is influenced by the amount of the proper biome for a species on the planet. Also, if an evolutionarily higher form of life appears, it will have an advantage over an advanced lower form of life.

All intelligent, sentient SimEarthlings act very much like humans in development of civilization, cities, industry, etc.

THE MONOLITH

The Monolith is a tool to help accelerate the advancement of intelligent species. It is an Evolution Speed-up Device (our thanks to Arthur C. Clark). Once you select the Monolith, if you click on a life-form, there is a one-in-three chance of that life-form suddenly mutating to a higher level, which immediately moves you to the next Time Scale. The Monolith won't work on all the animals. If you try to use the Monolith on the wrong animal, the program will beep at you, but there will be no energy charge. It costs 2500 E.U. to use a Monolith—whether or not it works.

A disadvantage to using the Monolith is that you could jump ahead into the civilization Time Scale before enough fossil fuels have been generated, and civilization will collapse. You need a wide population base to advance to the next technology level. Don't rush to a new Time Scale at the expense of your population.

INFLUENCING CIVILIZATION

The main way you influence your sentient life-forms is by telling them what energy sources to invest in, and how to allocate the energy. This is done through the CIVILIZATION MODEL CONTROL PANEL.

ENERGY

In SimEarth there are two uses of energy. You, the player, use it to make, mold, modify and manipulate the planet, and civilized SimEarthlings make and use it to carry on their daily lives.

The energy in SimEarth is measured in Energy Units, or E.U. The symbol Ω is used in the program as the symbol for an Energy Unit.

Intelligent SimEarthlings will produce and use energy. You can control their choice of energy sources and their use of the energy they produce, but you don't have *direct* access to *their* energy for *your* purposes.

Depending on the difficulty level of the game, you will have different amounts of energy to affect the planet and the simulation. These amounts are both your starting supply and the maximum you can accumulate at any one time.

If you are in experimental mode, you will have an unlimited supply of energy.

EXPERIMENTAL MODE   Unlimited Energy
EASY GAME   5000 E.U.
MEDIUM GAME   2000 E.U.
HARD GAME   2000 E.U.

Energy for a game comes from the stores of the planet itself in the form of geothermal, wind, and solar energy, as well as fossil fuels. As you deplete your energy supplies during a game, it will slowly build back up over time as the planet increases its energy from the above sources. This continual tapping of the planet's energies happens automatically.

The amount of energy you have to use is displayed in the EDIT WINDOW in the AVAILABLE ENERGY DISPLAY.

Your energy reserves are depleted by every action you take that affects the planet or simulation. New energy becomes available on the planet through time from various sources explained below. You can tap some of this new energy. It will automatically be added to your available energy each Time/Simulation cycle.

As technology develops, your sentient SimEarthlings generate energy for their own use. As technology on the planet advances, they generate more energy more efficiently.

You don't have direct access to the SimEarthlings' energy, but some of it will be automatically tapped and added to your reserves. The amount of energy automatically added to your reserves each Time/Simulation cycle increases with the increasing level of technology on your planet. The rate at which your energy reserves increase is as follows:

GEOLOGIC TIME SCALE		1 E.U. per cycle
EVOLUTION TIME SCALE		1 E.U. per cycle
CIVILIZATION TIME SCALE	Stone Age	2 E.U. per cycle
	Bronze Age	3 E.U. per cycle
	Iron Age	4 E.U. per cycle
TECHNOLOGY TIME SCALE	Industrial Age	5 E.U. per cycle
	Atomic Age	6 E.U. per cycle
	Information Age	7 E.U. per cycle
	Nanotech Age	8 E.U. per cycle

SOURCES OF ENERGY

There are five sources of energy in SimEarth.

BIOENERGY—Burning wood, animal power, plant power (farming), and work done by hand by the sentient species. Bioenergy gets more efficient through time because of better, more efficient farming tools, and scientific breakthroughs such as recycling biowaste into fuel. Using bioenergy releases CO_2 into the atmosphere, so it has a minor polluting effect.

SOLAR/WIND—Sun-drying of food and clothes, windmills, sailing ships, solar heating, wind-powered generators, solar electric cells, and satellites collecting solar energy. Improves in efficiency as technology advances.

HYDRO/GEO—Waterwheels, dams, steam power, hydroelectric power, and geothermal power. Improves in efficiency as technology advances.

FOSSIL FUEL—Coal made from long-dead animals. A by-product of burning fossil fuels is the release of greenhouse gases into the atmosphere.

NUCLEAR—Atomic reactors, bombs, etc. Atomic explosions release dust and radiation into the atmosphere.

ENERGY COSTS

There is no free lunch in SimEarth, and the price you pay for everything is energy.
Here is the price list.

PLACE PROKARYOTE	35	E.U.
PLACE EUKARYOTE	70	E.U.
PLACE RADIATE	105	E.U.
PLACE ARTHROPOD	140	E.U.
PLACE MOLLUSK	175	E.U.
PLACE FISH	210	E.U.
PLACE CETACEAN	245	E.U.
PLACE TRICHORDATE	280	E.U.
PLACE INSECT	315	E.U.
PLACE AMPHIBIAN	350	E.U.
PLACE REPTILE	385	E.U.
PLACE DINOSAUR	420	E.U.
PLACE AVIAN	455	E.U.
PLACE MAMMAL	490	E.U.
PLACE STONE AGE	500	E.U.
PLACE BRONZE AGE	1000	E.U.
PLACE IRON AGE	1500	E.U.
PLACE INDUSTRIAL AGE	2000	E.U.
PLACE ATOMIC AGE	2500	E.U.
PLACE INFORMATION AGE	3000	E.U.
PLACE NANOTECH AGE	3500	E.U.
PLACE BIOME FACTORY	500	E.U.
PLACE OXYGENATOR	500	E.U.
PLACE NO_2 GENERATOR	500	E.U.
PLACE VAPORATOR	500	E.U.
PLACE CO_2 GENERATOR	500	E.U.
PLACE MONOLITH	2500	E.U.
PLACE ICE METEOR	500	E.U.
TRIGGER ANY EVENT	50	E.U.
PLANT ANY BIOME	50	E.U.
SET ALTITUDE	50	E.U.
MOVE ANYTHING	30	E.U.
EXAMINE ANYTHING	5	E.U.
CHANGE CONTROL PANEL	30	E.U. per click
	150	E.U. per drag

SIMULATION
FLOW CHART

Inside the back cover of this manual is a flowchart that describes the inner workings of the SimEarth program.

Referring to this chart will be useful for solving problems and understanding what the simulation does and why it does it.

AN
INTRODUCTION
TO EARTH
SCIENCE

"The performance of a Prokaryote
is far superior to that of an
Amateurkaryote."

Maxwell Maxis

SimEarth

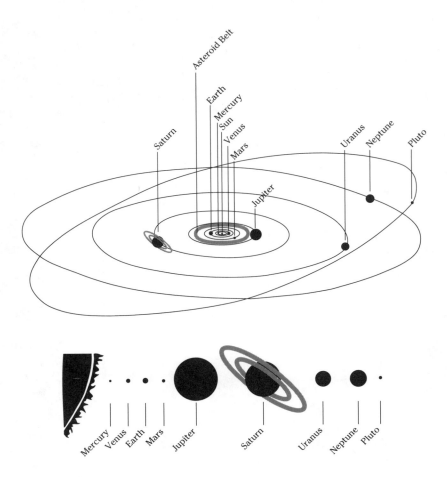

INTRODUCTION

SimEarth is a computer simulation of the Earth as a living system, developed in the spirit of James Lovelock's Gaia hypothesis. To get the most out of SimEarth, a little background in earth science is necessary.

This section of the manual is a primer to give you a start in understanding how our planet works. You will become familiar with many cause and effect relationships that are key to the dynamic play you will experience in SimEarth.

Figure 1 Our Solar System

In the last 30 years, more than 200 men and women from 18 nations have traveled in space and looked back at earth. These astronauts took beautiful pictures that provide a new look at our planet.

The view of Earth from space is having a deep impact on our culture: it is changing the way we look at our world and our place in it. It is a surprising view for those who came from a Western scientific background in which the study of the Earth was divided up into separate segments, and the Earth was viewed as a "dead" planet.

Earth science is a relatively recent approach to looking at our planet. It encompasses all the other sciences focused on understanding the Earth. It involves physics, chemistry, biology, astronomy, psychology, sociology and other areas of research. James Lovelock's Gaia hypothesis provides a framework for us to view the planet as a living system.

Earth is different from every other planet in our solar system.

EARTH AND THE OTHER PLANETS

Earth is the biggest of the four inner planets (Figure 1). It is the only planet with an atmosphere suitable for oxygen-breathing life. The Earth also has the biggest moon in proportion to its size in the Solar System: so big that some think we are a two-planet system.

No other planet (that we know of) has plate tectonics, a dynamic atmosphere and a hydrosphere. No other planet has an atmospheric composition like ours, nor the systems of life we have in our biosphere. This is not to say that other planets have no life in the broadest sense of the word, but not as we know it on Earth.

Earth scientists divide the earth into four interrelated components:

the **Lithosphere**—The solid, rocky part of the Earth: continents and ocean floor;
the **Hydrosphere**—the liquid part of the Earth: oceans, lakes and rivers;
the **Atmosphere**—the gaseous part of the Earth: air and clouds; and
the **Biosphere**—the living part of the Earth: humans, plants and animals.

Mercury is the closest planet to the Sun and so small that the light gases such as oxygen (O_2) and carbon dioxide (CO_2) evaporated during the planet's formation.

Venus has so much carbon dioxide (CO_2) that its surface temperature is more than 700° C—what is usually known as a runaway greenhouse effect. Venus probably had some plate tectonics in the past, but no longer.

Mars definitely had plate tectonics, volcanos, and mountains in the past, but being smaller than the Earth, it cooled more rapidly and is now geologically dead. The Martian atmosphere is so thin it would be impossible for humans to survive in it.

The rest of the Solar System, which includes Jupiter, Neptune, Saturn, Uranus and Pluto, are either so large or so far away from the Sun that they are too cold for life. They are mostly gaseous, unlike the rocky, solid inner planets.

ABOUT THIS INTRODUCTION TO EARTH SCIENCE

This Introduction to Earth Science is presented in five sections:

Geology (Lithosphere)
Climate (Atmosphere and Hydrosphere)
Life (Biosphere)
Humans and Civilizations (Biosphere)
Theories of the Earth

GEOLOGY

This section deals with the Lithosphere—the solid rocky part of the Earth. It covers the following subjects:

- the Origin of the Earth;
- the Evolution of the Earth;
- the Composition and Structure of the Earth;
- Special Characteristics of the Earth; and
- the Divisions of the Earth.

THE ORIGIN OF THE EARTH

How did our solar system come into existence? Scientists currently lean towards the **solar nebula hypothesis**.

This hypothesis states the following series of events:

A primordial cloud of gas and dust, called a nebula, once rotated in space.

The gravitational attraction of the material inside the nebula caused contraction of the primordial cloud, speeding up its rotation.

The shape changed to that of a flattened disk as a consequence of the increased rotation.

Matter then migrated towards the center, and formed what is called a **proto-Sun**.

The formation of the proto-Sun and the possible explosion of a nearby supernova caused the collapse of the nebula and triggered the formation of the solar system.

The collapse increased the temperature of the proto-Sun due to a thermonuclear chain reaction (high-temperature fusion of hydrogen atoms to form helium atoms).

The proto-Sun started to shine.

Matter began to form out of the material in space.

The hot proto-Sun and the surrounding gas and dust that still remained after the collapse began cooling down.

Gaseous material started to condense.

Small chunks of matter called planetesimals clumped together.

The biggest ones pulled most of the matter due to their higher gravitational attraction. If the **planetesimals** were too close to the Sun the lightest materials (hydrogen, helium, etc.) were blown away by the Sun's wind.

The planetesimals closest to the Sun were also composed of the densest materials (the ones with the highest melting points), like

iron. A good example is Mercury, with a density more than five times the density of water.

As the planetesimals got farther away from the Sun and therefore colder, lighter materials, such as silicon and oxygen, condensed and formed the rocky silicate planets (Venus, Mars, Earth).

The biggest and farthest-away planetesimals, which eventually became the giant planets Jupiter and Saturn, were able to retain the very light compounds such as hydrogen, methane and ammonia.

This hypothesis, although not completely tested, explains the basics of planetary formation and gives us the background to develop hypotheses for the evolution of the Earth from a condensed, homogeneous planetesimal to the differentiated, layered medium it is now.

THE EVOLUTION OF THE EARTH

THE FIRST BILLION YEARS

Age-dating of meteorites and the oldest rocks on the planet tell us that the oldest solid rocks on the Earth are about four billion years old, and that the Earth is about 4.7 billion years old.

Five billion years ago, what was later to become the Earth was a homogeneous conglomeration of silicon compounds, some iron, magnesium, and oxygen compounds, and smaller amounts of the other elements.

The pre-Earth was not as large as the planet we know today. It grew to its present size by the gradual addition of other planetesimals and meteorite bombardment.

The continuous bombardment not only increased the size of the planet, but it also heated it up. The rise in temperature due to impacts and gravitational compression, linked with the radioactive decay of heavy elements (which also produces heat), most likely partially melted the primordial Earth. The partially molten Earth was then affected by what is known as the **iron catastrophe**, which then led to the formation of the core.

FORMATION OF THE EARTH'S CORE

Within the partially molten primordial Earth, iron droplets, denser than the surrounding liquid, started falling towards the center of the planet forming a liquid iron core. Other dense elements (such as nickel and gold) followed. Since then, the Earth's core has been composed mainly of iron and nickel. Initially all liquid, it has slowly cooled from the center out, so that the Earth now has both an inner solid core and outer liquid core. The outer core, being liquid and very hot, convects (like boiling water in a pan), which generates the Earth's unique and strong magnetic field. The accumulation of iron at the center of the Earth released a large amount of energy that caused the rest of the Earth to melt.

DIFFERENTIATION AND THE FORMATION OF THE ATMOSPHERE AND OCEANS

The Earth, now almost completely molten, began a period of rapid differentiation.

The molten material, lighter than its surrounding solid parent, rose to the surface of the Earth and formed a primitive crust. It later separated into the lighter continental crust and the denser oceanic crust. The material left between the dense iron core in the center and the crust became the mantle.

Differentiation was also responsible for the initial escape of gases from the interior, called **outgassing**, which eventually led to the formation of the atmosphere and oceans.

Earth is made up of three main layers: the crust, the mantle and the core, as shown in Figures 2A and B.

CRUST

The **crust** is the uppermost layer of the Earth. There are two types of crust: **oceanic**, made of basalt, and **continental**, composed mostly of granite. Oceanic rock is dense, has deep trenches and varies from six to ten kilometers in thickness (the Marianas in the Pacific and the Puerto Rico trench in the Atlantic). Continental crust is 35 kilometers thick on average. The crust is rigid and elastic at the same time.

MANTLE

The **mantle** is divided into several layers and is separated from the crust by a discontinuity, or break, called the **Mohorovicic** ("Moho," for short). The **uppermost mantle** extends for approximately 100 km under the **Moho**, below the oceanic and continental crust. This part of the mantle is composed of mainly two minerals (olivine and pyroxene),

COMPOSITION AND STRUCTURE OF THE EARTH

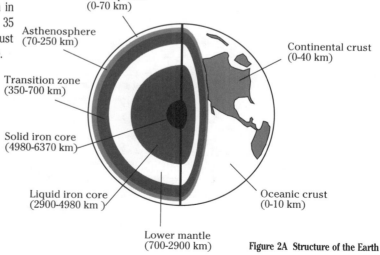

Lithosphere (0-70 km)

Asthenosphere (70-250 km)

Transition zone (350-700 km)

Solid iron core (4980-6370 km)

Liquid iron core (2900-4980 km)

Lower mantle (700-2900 km)

Continental crust (0-40 km)

Oceanic crust (0-10 km)

Figure 2A Structure of the Earth

and has the same rheological (deforming) properties as the crust: it is both rigid and elastic.

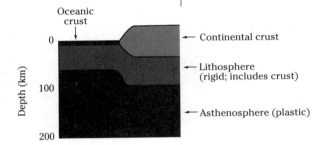

Figure 2B Structure of the Crust

Because they have the same rheological properties, the crust and uppermost mantle behave in unity.

Together, the crust and uppermost mantle comprise the **lithosphere,** which reaches down as far as 150 km below the surface. Surface **plate tectonics**, which are described later in the manual, explain the behavior of the lithosphere.

Below the lithosphere is the **asthenosphere**. This layer extends to a depth of 300 km below the surface of the earth.

Composed of the same materials as the uppermost mantle, the asthenosphere is considered a separate layer from the lithosphere because it behaves differently. The asthenosphere is hotter, weaker, and **plastic**: it deforms permanently under pressure. The hotter a material gets the less elastic and more plastic it becomes.

To give you an example with everyday materials, let's use a rubber band and toffee. An elastic rubber band stretches to a certain limit and then it breaks—a sudden, clean break. If we release it before it breaks it will go back to its original form. Toffee, on the other hand, will deform plastically under the same forces. If you pull on it, it stretches just like the rubber band, but if you release it before it breaks it will stay stretched or deformed; it will not bounce back to its original shape. The lithosphere acts like the rubber band, the asthenosphere like the toffee.

Below the asthenosphere is the **transition zone**, the area between 300 and 700 km beneath the surface. The transition zone, although hotter than the asthenosphere, is not partially molten.

The transition zone gets its name from the fact that the minerals (mainly olivine and pyroxene, but also some garnet) transform to denser forms within this region due to heat and pressure. They reach their most dense possible structure at 700 km, the boundary between the upper mantle (lithosphere, asthenosphere and transition zone) and the **lower mantle**.

The lower mantle extends from 700 km to 2700 km below the surface of the Earth. From 2700 to 2900 km is another transition region that separates the mantle and the core.

CORE

The center of the Earth is called the **core** and has two layers. The outer core, comprised of iron and nickel, extends from 2900 to 5120 km beneath the surface. The outer core is liquid and hot. The motion of the fluid in this region generates the Earth's unique and strong magnetic field.

The inner core begins at 5120 km and extends to the center of the Earth, 6400 km below the surface. The temperature at the center of the Earth is about 10,000° C—hotter than the surface of the Sun.

The Earth possesses unique characteristics that separate it from the rest of the planets: a powerful magnetic field, the presence of plate tectonics which have changed the surface structure significantly over time, and the existence of an atmosphere, oceans and life.

SPECIAL CHARACTERISTICS OF THE EARTH

MAGNETIC FIELD

By slow convective movements in the liquid iron core, electric currents are produced in the core which generate and maintain the Earth's magnetic field.

The magnetic field is what enables us to navigate the seas or find our way through a deep forest by using a compass. In simple terms, the Earth's magnetic field can be described as a giant magnet with North and South poles. The North magnetic pole coincides with the geographic North pole.

At certain points in time, the magnetic field reverses—the magnetic North becomes South and magnetic South becomes North. By examining very old rocks with magnetic minerals that preserve the orientation of the magnetic field at the time they formed, geologists have been able to construct the **magnetic polarity time scale**, key in the development of the theory of **sea-floor spreading** and plate tectonics. The last magnetic field reversal was over a million years ago.

PLATE TECTONICS AND CONVECTION

The Earth is also unique in that its surface layer, the lithosphere, is broken up into pieces, or plates, that move and deform. The movement and deformation of the plates—plate tectonics—is responsible for mountain building, earthquakes and volcanos. There are 12 major plates on the planet, illustrated in Figure 3.

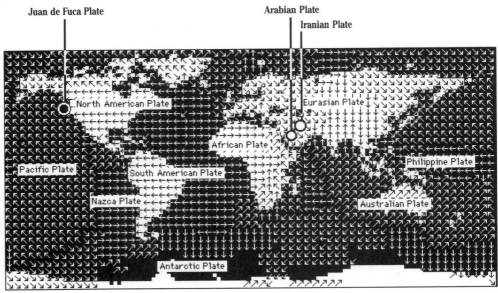

Figure 3 Tectonic Map of the Earth's
Surface

The plates move in response to the convection of the mantle underneath. Convection is a mechanism of heat transfer in which hot material from the bottom rises to the top (hotter material is less dense and therefore weighs less), and the cooler surface material sinks. Convection is the most effective form of heat transport.

ATMOSPHERE, OCEANS, AND LIFE

Another important characteristic of the Earth is its fluid sphere: the atmosphere and oceans. Earth is the only planet in which two-thirds of the surface is covered by water, and is surrounded by an atmosphere composed mostly of oxygen and nitrogen. These two features have enabled the Earth to develop an amazing variety of living organisms.

There are many theories for the origin of the atmosphere and oceans. The most widely accepted theory states that in the Earth's earliest beginnings, it had no gaseous atmosphere. It was too small, and didn't have enough gravity to retain the lighter gaseous elements that existed at that time.

As time passed, the Earth increased in size and mass: large meteorites and planetesimals added their mass by crashing into the Earth, and the Earth's gravity attracted smaller particles of matter. Eventually, Earth was big enough to retain an atmosphere.

The original atmospheric gases (very different from today's oxygen-nitrogen atmosphere) must have been produced by outgassing (the escape of gases from within the solid planetary mass) during the initial differentiation.

This early atmosphere must have had a similar composition to the gases released during volcanic eruptions today, and consisted of water vapor, hydrogen, hydrogen chlorides, carbon dioxide and monoxide, and nitrogen. The light hydrogen compounds could not and cannot be held by Earth's gravity, and so they must have escaped away as they do today. As the planet cooled, the water vapor in the atmosphere condensed into the water that formed the oceans.

The present atmospheric composition was achieved later by several chemical reactions and the evolution of life.

INFLUENCE OF THE SUN AND MOON

The presence of the Moon has one major visible effect on the Earth: most notably, the behavior of the oceans in the form of tides. The gravitational pull of the Moon and the Sun on the Earth causes the sea level to alternately rise and fall during the day. Gravitational effects are observed in both the oceans and the solid Earth, though the latter can only be detected by very sensitive instruments.

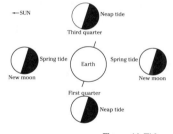

Figure 4A Tides

The tides in the water can be seen and measured accurately and the time of occurrence calculated. The side of the Earth facing the Moon feels the strongest tide and the side opposite to it feels the minimum tide. As the Earth rotates, the tides move around it. The Sun, although farther away, is so large that it has the same effect. Solar tides are half the height of lunar tides, and are not in phase with the lunar tides. Solar tides occur every 24 hours; lunar tides occur every six hours (high, low, high, low).

When the Earth, Moon and Sun line up the tides are very strong. These are called spring tides and they occur every two weeks, at full and new Moon. When the Moon and the Sun are at right angles to each other with respect to the Earth we have the lowest tides, known as neap tides, which occur between first- and third-quarter moons.

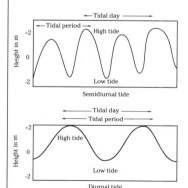

Figure 4B

Tides cause loss of energy through friction between the water and the sea floor. The energy loss is enough to slow down the rotation of the Earth by a very small amount. This effectively lengthens the day. All these patterns are shown in Figure 4.

DIVISIONS OF THE EARTH

We can summarize the behavior of the Earth in a fairly concise way by dividing its processes in two: surface processes of the external heat engine and internal processes of the internal heat engine.

A heat engine is a mechanism that converts high-temperature heat (energy) into work. It is composed of four main "parts":
1) High T (temperature) source;
2) Working fluid;
3) Work to be done; and
4) Low T sink (something that cools by absorbing heat).

These parts in the internal and external heat engines are identified below.

	EXTERNAL HEAT ENGINE	INTERNAL HEAT ENGINE
SOURCE	Radiation from the Sun	Heat from radioactive decay
		Latent heat from fusion of the core
WORKING FLUID	Atmosphere and oceans	Mantle rocks
WORK	Erosion, weathering, etc.	Plate tectonics
SINK	Outer space	Outer space

EXTERNAL HEAT ENGINE

Many of the surface processes of the Earth are the direct result of the work done by the external heat engine. These processes are what determine many, but not all, of the short- and long-term changes in the Earth's landscape.

The processes that occur within the external heat engine can be classified into four groups:

Erosion: the set of processes that results in the loosening of soil and rock, as well as its removal downhill or downwind.

Weathering: the set of processes, chemical or physical, that results in the breakup and decay of bedrock. Of the four processes, this is now the most important for human concerns. Weathering breaks up and chemically changes bedrock, transforming it into soil essential for agriculture. Our abusive agricultural system is eroding good soil at a rate faster than it can be created by weathering.

Transportation: the set of processes involved in moving loosened material from one place to another.

Deposition: the set of processes resulting in the settling down of the transported sediment.

These four processes are carried out by three main agents: **wind**, **water** and **glaciers**.

WIND

Wind is an important agent of erosion and deposition. In deserts, for example, all the erosion, transportation and deposition of sand is exclusively carried out by winds. Normal winds can only carry very small particles, but strong winds, as in the Sahara sandstorms, can carry a markedly heavier load.

WATER

Water in its fluid form is the most important agent of erosion, transport and deposition on the surface of the Earth. Water is also important in chemical and physical weathering as it is the fluid that enables many of the chemical reactions that break down bedrock; it also enlarges cracks in the freezing and thawing processes.

Water causes erosion of soil by runoff after heavy rain, in river channels from the head to the mouth (mostly at the head), and by ocean currents both along coasts and on the bottom of the ocean. Water in rivers is extremely important in shaping the landscape, i.e., the Grand Canyon and the Colorado River.

Transport of sediments by water occurs in runoff channels, in rivers and in currents in the ocean or along the shore.

Water allows deposition of sediment in river channels and deltas. Deposition by water is very clearly seen in the inside part of the curves of rivers, in deltas, and also in the ocean bottom as a river enters the ocean and dumps its sediment load on the bigger body of water.

Water reservoirs on land are rivers, groundwater and lakes. Glaciers are also a reservoir of water, but they will be treated separately.

GLACIERS

Large bodies of water accumulated as ice are usually known as glaciers. There are several types of glaciers: mountain glaciers like those that covered Yosemite in California, continent-sized glaciers known as ice-sheets like those in Greenland or Antarctica, and others.

Glaciers are a very powerful and rapid agent of erosion, transport and deposition. Glaciers can carve a valley in a shorter time scale than any river. They can transport sediment that ranges from sand grains to boulders the size of a house.

Glacier landscapes are recognized by their U-shaped valleys, while river valleys are V-shaped. The valley floors have striations caused by the boulders scraping the bedrock, and the sides and end of the valley have an assortment of rock sizes we generally call moraines.

OTHER SURFACE PROCESSES
Two hot topics of public debate are the processes and effects of **global warming** and **air pollution**. The following section will lend insight into these topics as we discuss the basics of the **carbon cycle** and **element transport** by rivers to the oceans.

THE CARBON CYCLE
Carbon dioxide (CO_2) is used by **photosynthetic** organisms (organisms that make their own food) such as plants, to generate the complex carbohydrates and the energy they need for survival. In this process the carbon is locked up in complex molecules and oxygen is returned to the atmosphere.

Non-photosynthetic organisms such as humans and other animals breathe oxygen and give back CO_2 to the atmosphere. When either type of organism dies, the organic matter decays and the carbon in the complex molecules is released generally in the form of CO_2.

Carbon also accumulates to form fossil fuels that humans have learned to use. Such burning of the carbon in these fuels releases additional CO_2 into the atmosphere, causing an unbalance or destabilization in the natural equilibrium of the atmosphere/biosphere dynamic relationship.

Cutting down forests or plants also creates a destabilization of the environment, because it results in less photosynthesis. As a result, less CO_2 is consumed and less oxygen is produced.

The highest reservoir of carbon is found in rocks, especially in limestone. The carbon is trapped in the limestone when marine organisms, whose shells are made of calcite, die and fall to the bottom of the ocean and accumulate into thick layers. When the layers compact and harden they become limestone. Most of the carbon stays there until the ocean floor, and the limestone with it, is consumed through earthquake and volcanic activity. Then the limestone melts and the carbon in the form of CO_2 gas is released through volcanos and returned to the atmosphere.

The processes of weathering and erosion cause many elements trapped in minerals to be transported back to the oceans, where they interact with both the oceanic water and rocks.

For the purposes of studying the Earth, we need to know how these elements are transported back to the oceans and how long they interact with water before being trapped in minerals. This helps us understand mountain-building activity, the measure of erosion rates, and how rock/water interactions and basalt composition form the oceans.

For environmental reasons, knowledge of these processes is equally important. It teaches us about the behavior of toxic or radioactive elements in the ocean that occur, for example, as a result of disasters such as major oil spills. It also helps us understand the effects of increased CO_2 in the atmosphere, which occurs as a result of the burning of fossil fuels by an ever-increasing population.

INTERNAL HEAT ENGINE— PLATE TECTONICS

The most outstanding achievement of the Earth sciences in all its history was the advent of the theory of plate tectonics in the 1960s, which, with a few simple geometrical arguments, has organized and explained the large-scale processes of the surface of the Earth.

Plate tectonics is the work done by the internal heat engine.

HISTORY

Early in the 1600s Sir Francis Bacon had already noticed the jigsaw-puzzle features of the early maps produced by the explorers of the New World. Later, Antonio Snider and Edouard Suess proposed the existence of a giant super-continent, but it was not until the late 1920s, 100 years after their first publication, that a hypothesis explaining these features was proposed.

In 1929, Alfred Wegener, a meteorologist, proposed the Continental Drift hypothesis. Wegener collected paleontological data on fossil plants and animals in the Old and New worlds, as well as other geological evidence (structures, rock types and ages across the equatorial Atlantic) and proposed the existence of a giant supercontinent that broke into the present continents 200 million years ago. He named this continent **Pangaea**.

Wegener's hypothesis was dismissed after 10 years because he failed to present a valid mechanism that would satisfy the physicists and geophysicists of the time. Ironically, 60 years later, continental drift and plate tectonics are accepted as the ruling paradigm of the earth sciences, but there still isn't a clear idea of the mechanism that causes it.

Continental drift and plate tectonics were finally accepted in the 1960s after several geologists and geophysicists presented incontrovertible evidence of sea-floor spreading, ocean consumption and transform motions.

PLATE TECTONICS

In simple terms, the earth's surface is not continuous and static, but broken into pieces like a giant jigsaw puzzle. Those pieces can be continental or oceanic. They move due to flow in the mantle underneath the surface. With this simple explanation, plate tectonics was used to explain the distribution and nature of volcanos around the Pacific Ring of Fire and also the distribution of earthquakes all around the world.

Plate tectonics is the theory that explains how the lithosphere is broken into pieces called spherical caps that are internally rigid and change in limited amounts only at boundaries. Three types of boundaries exist: divergent (mid-ocean ridges), convergent (subduction zones), and transform (faults). The caps move at constant velocities which are continually being determined by the convection in the mantle.

Before we explain the three different types of boundaries, or margins, what follows is an explanation of volcanos and earthquakes.

VOLCANOS

A volcano is a land edifice that is slowly built up by the eruption of hot molten rock (**magma**) on the surface of the Earth. The erupted rocks, made up of many different compositions (cooled magma) are called volcanic. If the molten rocks don't reach the surface, but cool under the volcano, they are called plutonic.

The hot magma flowing on the surface is called lava. Volcanos can be of very different types depending on the composition of the rocks. The composition determines if the volcanos will erupt quietly (Kilauea, Hawaii) or violently (Mt. Saint Helens, Washington).

Volcanos occur at two plate boundaries and also in the middle of plates. When associated with convergent boundaries, they are usually violent; when divergent they are under water and erupt quietly. Intra-plate volcanos are often associated with hot-spots in the bottom of the mantle that produce chains of volcanos such as we find in Hawaii. These are usually quiet volcanos.

Knowing the plate boundaries is important in predicting which type of eruption will occur so that volcanic hazards can be properly evaluated. Big, violent eruptions can send so much material into the atmosphere that it will change the color of sunsets or cool the global temperature by a few degrees. This happened in the 1880s when Krakatoa erupted in Indonesia. The sunsets were intensely red for a year and England did not have a summer for two years.

EARTHQUAKES

An earthquake is the result of the sudden release of energy that has been accumulating between two parts of the Earth divided by a fracture we know as a **fault**. The energy accumulates because the two sides of the fault cannot slide past each other easily; rather, they find a lot of resistance to sliding and this resistance locks the fault. When the resistance is higher than the blocks can stand, the fault snaps and an earthquake occurs.

Earthquake magnitude is measured by the Richter scale, which is a measure of the energy released by the earthquake. What we feel is measured by a subjective scale of intensity called the Mercalli scale. Earthquakes occur at all three plate boundaries because they all divide blocks of the Earth, where there is resistance to sliding.

Earthquakes occur below the surface of the earth but are located by latitude and longitude measurements. Such measurements, which act like a grid around the entire surface of the Earth, are used to define an earthquake **epicenter**. The depth of the earthquake is called a **focus** or **hypocenter**. Earthquakes are classified by their depths into shallow (0–70 km), intermediate (70–300 km) and deep (300–700 km). Big, shallow earthquakes like those on the San Andreas fault are highly destructive.

DIVERGENT MARGINS

In the 1950s it was discovered that in the middle of the oceans there were very long mountain chains emitting volcanic material. These chains, known as Mid-Ocean Ridges, are where new oceanic floor (basalt) is constantly being created. The material builds up symmetrically on both sides of the ridge with a deep central valley. There are volcanos and shallow earthquakes there. This type of boundary is called a **constructive boundary** because sea-floor material is generated here. Figure 5 illustrates these features.

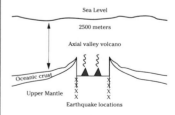

Figure 5 Divergent Plate Margin

Mid-ocean ridges can be followed for a continuous 40,000 km from the Atlantic to the Pacific, the Indian Ocean and so on.

TRANSFORM MARGINS

The ridges are offset by faults known as transform faults. These faults are plate boundaries that join ridges to ridges, ridges to trenches, faults to trenches, and so on. Material is not created nor destroyed at transform faults. They are vertical faults that generate shallow earthquakes. The best example is the San Andreas fault. This type of margin is illustrated in Figure 6.

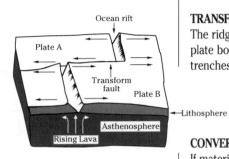

Figure 6 Transform Margin

CONVERGENT MARGINS

If material is created at the ridges and the Earth is not getting bigger, ocean crust must be destroyed somewhere. This occurs at convergent margins, also known as **subduction zones**. Here an oceanic plate dives into the mantle under another younger and lighter oceanic plate or continental plate, such as with the Pacific oceanic plate under the continental South America. A continental plate cannot subduct, so when two continents converge they crash together in what is known as a continental collision, generating large mountain chains, such as the Himalayas.

Subduction of an oceanic plate generates magma, which rises under the overriding plate and builds a volcanic line such as what takes place in the Andes. Subduction generates 99% of the seismic energy released every year, in shallow, intermediate, and deep earthquakes. It also generates the biggest earthquakes (9.5 on the Richter scale in Chile, 1960; 9.0 in Alaska, 1964). Convergent margins are illustrated in Figure 7.

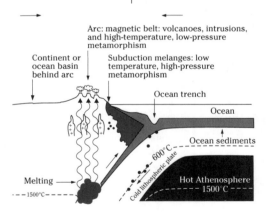

Figure 7 Convergent Margin

CLIMATE

The study of atmospheric and hydrospheric systems (air and oceans) explains the climate of the planet. The greenhouse effect and other present-day environmental problems are related to climate. Climate is part of the external heat engine and is driven by the radiational energy of the Sun.

ATMOSPHERE

The composition of our atmosphere is shown in Table 1. It is composed of 78% nitrogen gas (N_2), 21% oxygen (O_2), about .93% argon (A), and minor amounts of carbon dioxide (CO_2). There are also traces of nitrous oxide (NO_2), methane (CH_4) and sulfur dioxide (SO_2).

The atmosphere did not always have this composition—free oxygen was not available until the first photosynthetic organisms appeared. This will be covered later in the chapter on "Life."

The atmosphere is divided into four layers: **troposphere**, **stratosphere**, **mesosphere** and **thermosphere**. The four layers are mentioned in ascending order from the bottom to the top of the atmospheric column in Figure 8.

Figure 8 also shows the temperature gradient in the atmosphere, as well as the position of the ozone layer. Ozone (O_3) is a compound of oxygen that absorbs and repels a large percentage of the ultraviolet radiation in solar energy.

The ozone layer protects us from the deadly UV rays of the Sun's radiation. Our use of chlorofluorocarbons enlarges the hole in the ozone layer, which reduces this protection.

GAS	CHEMICAL SYMBOL	CONTENT (% by volume)
Nitrogen	N_2	78.09
Oxygen	O_2	20.95
Argon	A	0.93
Carbon dioxide	CO_2	0.03
Total		100.00

Table 1 Principal Components of Dry Air

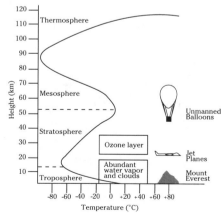

Figure 8 Structure and Temperature of the Atmosphere

OCEANS

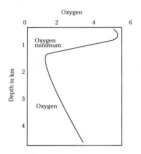

Figure 9 Oxygen Content of the Oceans

Not just composed of water, oceans have many other elements in solution such as sodium, potassium, and calcium, and gases such as carbon dioxide (see Table 2). All of the dissolved elements are critical for the survival of marine plants and animals.

Life in the deep oceans is limited greatly by the availability of food and light. The zone of the ocean that is well-lighted is called the **euphotic zone** (upper 200 meters) and the darker, deeper layers are called the **aphotic zone**. The amount of oxygen available in the oceans also decreases sharply at deeper levels, as shown in Figure 9.

The structure of the oceans detailed in the figure below shows that water temperature decreases to 4° C at a depth of 2000 meters in tropical and temperate regions. The temperature and salinity gradients in the oceanic column are shown in Figure 10.

Figure 10A Surface Temperature of the Oceans

ELEMENT	AMOUNT IN OCEAN (G)	RESIDENCE IN TIME (YR)
Sodium	147×10^{20}	260,000,000
Magnesium	18×10^{20}	12,000,000
Potassium	5.3×10^{20}	11,000,000
Calcium	5.6×10^{20}	1,000,000
Silicon	5.2×10^{18}	8,000
Manganese	1.4×10^{15}	700
Iron	1.4×10^{16}	140
Aluminum	1.4×10^{16}	100

Table 2 Residence Time of Some Elements in Seawater

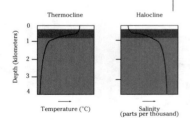

Figure 10B Temperature and Salinity of the Oceans with Depth

The energy to carry out processes on the surface of the Earth comes from the Sun. Solar radiation, also known as **insolation**, is what spurs life and geological processes on the Earth.

SOLAR HEATING —INSOLATION

Since the birth of the Solar System, the Sun has been radiating heat at a constantly increasing rate. This is the natural consequence of the growth of a star. The life span of a star like the Sun is about 1400 billion years, which means that the Sun will last for approximately another 10 billion years. The solar radiation will increase with time and cause the surface temperature of the Earth to get higher and higher until the Sun dies. When this finally happens, life on the Earth will probably die unless forms of life not dependent on photosynthesis evolve.

Climate is highly dependent on solar output variations. Seasons (winter and summer) and climatic zones are dependent on solar output. Figure 11 shows the angle of the Earth to the solar rays with different seasons and at different latitudinal zones. Variations in solar output do not follow just the seasonal cycle of summer and winter. They also follow other longer cycles that are directly related to long-period changes in temperature on the Earth, such as during glaciations.

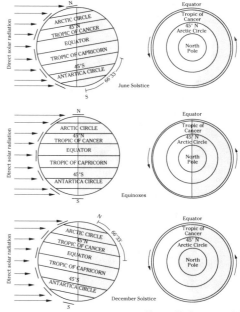

Figure 11 Exposure of the Earth to the Sun's Radiation

Scientists have argued for a long time on the cause of the recent (10,000 to 15,000 years ago) ice ages since they were discovered by Louis Agassiz in the 1800s.

GLACIATIONS AND CHANGES IN THE ORBIT OF THE EARTH

In the 1930s, a mathematically sound hypothesis for glaciation and long-period climate changes was proposed by Milutin Milankovitch, a Yugoslavian astronomer. He proposed the astronomical theory of climate, which says that variations in the Earth's orbit influence climate by changing the seasonal and latitudinal distribution of incoming solar radiation.

Incoming solar radiation falls at different angles in different seasons. The angle of incidence depends on the tilt of the rotation axis of the Earth (**axial tilt**). This tilt is technically called **obliquity**, and is measured with respect to a plane that crosses the Sun and contains the orbit of the Earth (plane of the ecliptic).

Another factor that influences the angle of incidence of solar radiation is the **precession**, or the measure of how the equinoxes succeed each other and how this affects the seasonal configuration of the Earth. Precession depends on the longitude of the perihelion (the point at which the Earth is closer to the Sun).

A final factor that influences the angle of incidence of solar radiation is **eccentricity**, which is a measure of how much the orbit of the Earth around the Sun differs from a perfect circle.

Obliquity, eccentricity and precession of the equinoxes are called the **orbital parameters**, and variations in them determine changes in the solar heating and therefore affect our climate. These parameters cause changes with different period lengths:

Eccentricity	Long-period cycles	95,000; 136,000; 413,000 years
Obliquity	Medium-period cycles	41,000 years
Precession	Short-period cycles	19,000; 23,000 years

Changes in climate are classified according to the lengths of their cycles:

Tectonic band	More than 400,000 years
Milankovitch band	10,000 to 400,000 years
Millenium band	400 to 10,000 years
Decadal band	10 to 400 years
Interannual band	2.5 to 10 years
Annual band	0.5 to 2.5 years

Changes in the tectonic band are attributed to tectonic effects such as mountain building. This is a current topic of research in paleoclimatology and is known as **Tectoclimatology**.

Changes in the Milankovitch band are due to changes in the orbital parameters mentioned above. These changes are the direct result of the gravitational pull of the giant planets (Jupiter and Saturn) on the Earth.

Changes in the millenium band are attributed to episodes of flux of volcanic gases, and expansion and contraction of alpine glaciers. Changes in the millenium band are due to episodes of explosive volcanism.

Finally, changes in the annual and interannual band are attributed to the well-known seasonal fluctuations of solar radiation. These are probably due to motions of the Earth around its own orbit (wobbling of the axis of rotation, for example) and not the geometry of the orbit as in the orbital parameters.

A variation in the solar output that frequently occurs is related to sunspot cycles. A sunspot is a dark area of the sun's surface, which represents a region of lower temperature than the rest of the sun's surface. Sunspot cycles are fluctuations in the ultraviolet radiation from the Sun. The approximate duration of a cycle is 11 years. The influence of sunspot cycles on the climate is still a controversial and constantly debated topic.

EARTH'S RESPONSE TO SOLAR HEATING

The Earth does not just passively absorb the radiation from the Sun, but returns some of the radiation back to space. It does not emit it back at the same frequency, but at a lower one. Emissions from the Earth are in the infrared spectrum while radiation from the Sun comes from the whole spectrum of light, from UV (ultraviolet) rays to visible to IR (infrared). The light spectrum is shown in Figure 12.

Part of the solar radiation (UV rays) is absorbed by the ozone layer, part is reflected by clouds and solids, part is absorbed by water vapor, dust particles and clouds, and 47% is absorbed by the ground. This is shown in Figure 13.

The overall albedo is the most important process preventing the Sun from frying us. It is measured by the amount of the Sun's radiant energy that is reflecting off clouds, water and land surfaces. This reflectivity is called **albedo**. Table 3 shows the albedo of several solid and fluid materials.

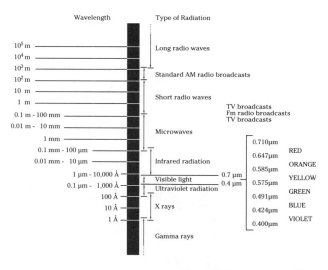

Figure 12 The Electromagnetic Spectrum

ALBEDO EFFECTS

SURFACE	%
Fresh snow, high sun	80-85
Fresh snow, low sun	90-95
Old snow	50-60
Sand	20-30
Grass	20-25
Dry earth	15-25
Wet earth	10
Forest	5-10
Water (sun near horizon)	50-80
Water (sun near zenith)	3-5
Thick cloud	70-80
Thin cloud	25-50
Planetary albedo	30
Ice	50-70
Fields dry	20-25
Fields green	3-15

Table 3 Albedo of Various Surfaces

Albedo is the ratio of light reflected to light received. The combination of the following mechanisms gives the total albedo of Earth and atmosphere.

Orbiting satellites keep track of the albedo in order to monitor the rate at which the earth's surface is heating when exposed to the sun. Such instruments measure short-wave and infrared radiation, both coming in from the sun and going out from the atmosphere and the earth's surface below. The earth's average albedo has been estimated at between 29% and 34%.

There are four major mechanisms for returning radiation to space:

• Reflection from dust, salt, ash and smoke particles in the air;
• Reflection from clouds;
• Reflection from the ground; and
• Refraction by air molecules.

If a ray reaches the Earth after all these obstacles then it still has to deal with the Earth's albedo. This varies depending on the composition of the surface. The average surface albedo is only 4% but in certain areas, for example the poles, the albedo is between 50–70%. Some of these values are tabulated in Table 3.

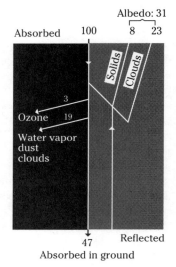

Figure 13 Solar Energy Budget

Because of its high albedo, the amount of snow that falls in a year will affect the climate and the average temperature of the Earth. The presence of more deserts will have the same effect. Deforestation, even though its albedo is very low, also affects the weather because more dry uncovered land with a high albedo gets exposed. The Earth retains this heat and transports it from equatorial latitudes to polar latitudes.

HEAT TRANSPORT & ATMOSPHERE-OCEAN INTERACTIONS

The heat absorbed by the ground and by the ocean surface waters is greater at the equator than at the poles because of the higher amount of insolation at these regions. This heat is transported from the equator to the poles both by the atmosphere and by the oceans. In a general sense, the atmosphere does it using winds and convection cells (like the mantle in the internal heat engine), and the oceans using currents, both surface and deep.

ATMOSPHERIC TRANSPORT

Atmospheric transport, or global circulation, takes place largely due to winds. The pattern of global circulation is characterized by permanent anticyclones and cyclones, called centers of action, and by persistent wind systems.

At low latitudes near the Earth's surface, the easterly trade winds dominate. At high latitudes and aloft, the prevailing westerlies dominate. The occurrence of zonal winds is explained by the deflection of motions of the meridians due to the rotation of the Earth. This is the **Coriolis effect**, which also says that particles in the Northern hemisphere tend to go to the right and in the Southern hemisphere to the left. The driving force for this circulation is the variation in solar radiation with latitude.

Near the surface of the Earth the pressure is low at the equator and high at the poles. This gives rise to a circulation along the meridians, with the heated air rising near the equator and flowing high towards the pole and the cooled air descending at high latitudes and flowing towards the equator at the ground. The stream of air moving towards the pole is deflected to the east by the Coriolis force, originating westerly winds, and the one flowing towards the equator at the ground will be deflected to generate the easterlies. Friction with the surface of the Earth does not allow the pressure and Coriolis force to balance so that the circulation is not just zonal but also along the meridians.

The pattern of meridional circulation was discovered by George Hadley in the 1700s and the circulation patterns along the meridians are called Hadley cells. Since friction does not allow pressure and Coriolis force to balance, the pressure force is greater at great heights than the Coriolis force and the air at great heights is pushed towards the poles. At high latitude the air tends to cool and descend, completing the meridional Hadley cell shown in Figure 14.

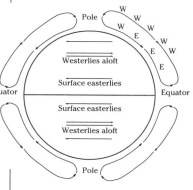

Figure 14 Hadley Cells

The Hadley cells, one in each hemisphere, perform the function of transferring excess heat from the Sun at low latitudes to higher latitudes. The true circulation pattern is not as simple as just having a Hadley cell in each hemisphere because of a law of physics called conservation of angular momentum. The results of applying the law show that Hadley cells alone will cause very high-speed winds, which in turn will cause great instability in the global circulation pattern. Friction between the Earth and the atmosphere also complicates simple Hadley cells.

Heat is also transported by waves and vortices. Waves in the atmosphere are the result of the breakdown of the zonal flow due to high-speed winds and lateral

mixing of the air. Swirls or vortices and cyclones and anticyclones also result from the breakdown of the zonal flow. These are very effective at transporting the heat in the North-South direction.

OCEANIC TRANSPORT

Heat transport from solar radiation is also accomplished via oceanic circulation. Circulation of the oceans is one of the main factors in the total heat budget of the Earth.

Oceans act as a great reservoir of heat for the planet. The Sun's energy heats up the surface of the ocean, which stores the heat and transports it via oceanic currents both at the surface and at depth. Like the atmosphere, the ocean currents move heat from low latitude to high latitudes.

HEAT STORAGE

The oceans are very large reservoirs of water that can hold a lot of heat without changing their average surface temperature by very much. This is known as the **climatic flywheel**.

Oceans are better at holding heat than the ground or the air, and absorb more heat per unit area at the equators than at the poles. The heat is transferred to the colder areas by convection. This moderating effect on the climate is easily observed in temperate coastal regions where warm air from the seas is transferred to the land.

SURFACE CURRENTS

The wind-driven circulation of the oceans is strong, but extends only within the upper 1000 meters of the ocean. The wind system described in the previous sections exerts a stress on the surface of the ocean, generating surface currents. The easterly trade winds form the equatorial currents of all oceans.

When intersected by land these currents are deflected North and South, as in the Atlantic and Pacific oceans. Deflected currents travel along the western parts of the oceans and are called western boundary currents—they are the strongest in all the oceans. One is the Gulf Stream.

These currents are driven by the westerly winds across the ocean and form currents that flow back into the equatorial region, completing the convection cell, similar to what occurs in atmospheric circulation. These cells or **gyres** occur in subtropical regions in the N and S Pacific, N and S Atlantic and S Indian oceans. The N and S gyres are separated by a countercurrent that flows east.

In the N Indian Ocean a similar gyre is found, but this changes direction every six months due to reversals in atmospheric circulation called **monsoons**. Some weaker gyres are found in northern subpolar regions. In southern gyres the flow is not blocked by land, so the Antarctic circumpolar flows completely around the world. The circulation is driven by differences in pressures between high and low areas of the sea surface.

The action of the wind on the surface of the ocean also causes vertical motion. These vertical currents are called upwellings and occur when prevailing winds blow parallel to a coast. These upwellings are in offshore and subsurface waters, which frequently are rich in nutrients. When this is the case, an area of high biological productivity may develop.

DEEP CURRENTS

Variations in water density cause deep water circulation known as **thermohaline circulation**. These density differences develop at the air-sea interface and are the result of differences in the amount of heat received and the effects of dilution and evaporation. The dense, cold waters of high latitudes sink and slowly flow towards the equator. This is a convective process, like that of the mantle inside the Earth. This process occurs principally in two places, the North Atlantic and the Antarctic.

The North Atlantic Deep Water is very clearly defined by its temperature, oxygen content and salinity. The Antarctic Bottom Water travels north along the ocean floor across the equator. The bottom water path is influenced by the topography of the ocean floor.

ATMOSPHERE-OCEAN INTERACTION

The interaction between ocean and atmosphere is shown in Figure 15, the hydrologic cycle. This cycle can be summarized as follows: the wind blowing over surface waters generates waves, mixes the surface waters and removes water vapor from the sea surface. The water vapor is taken into the atmosphere by evaporation and transferred to land by precipitation, which returns it to the rivers and groundwater that eventually return it to the sea.

Figure 15 Ocean-Atmosphere Interactions

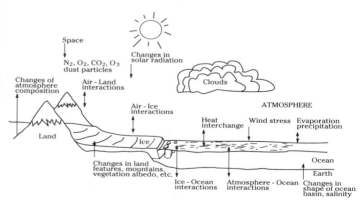

GREENHOUSE EFFECT

In recent years we have heard a lot about global warming and the greenhouse effect due to increasing consumption of fossil fuels and continuous deforestation, but few accurately know what the greenhouse effect is and how to gauge its delicate balance on the Earth. Not even the experts can predict the Earth's behavior in terms of global warming trends, because we don't know enough about climatic fluctuations and CO_2 levels in the past.

The greenhouse effect can be described as follows:

The atmosphere of the Earth is fairly transparent to the incoming visible rays of the Sun, but 48% of the radiation is absorbed by the ground and emitted back as infrared radiation. The atmosphere is opaque to infrared because carbon dioxide and water vapor absorb the radiation instead of allowing it to go back into space. This absorbed radiation heats the atmosphere, which radiates heat back to the Earth. Without this effect the Earth's surface temperature would be below freezing and the oceans a mass of ice.

Figure 16 CO_2 Levels in the Past

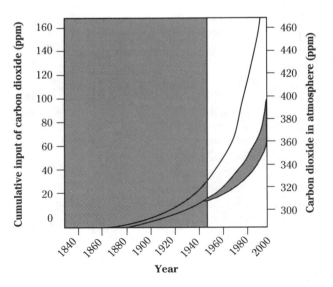

Any process that alters the delicate balance of CO_2 and water vapor molecules may affect Earth's climate. Burning fossil fuels increases the amount of CO_2 in the atmosphere, and deforestation of the Amazons prevents plants from taking CO_2 and returning oxygen to the atmosphere.

Since the beginning of the Industrial Revolution the amount of CO_2 in the atmosphere has increased steadily to values that we think have never been reached before (Figure 16 shows the increase since 1840 and predictions for the future). Some of these CO_2 molecules are taken from the atmosphere and dissolved in the oceans, because nature tries to reestablish equilibrium, but we are releasing so much CO_2 that the planet cannot rebalance itself.

Increases in global temperature caused by the greenhouse effect may also increase sea levels by 70 meters or more by melting part of the Antarctic ice sheet. This could be devastating to many coastal cities.

CLOUD COVER

We have already discussed briefly the effect of cloud cover on albedo and therefore on insolation. Cloud cover also affects the reflection of incoming rays from the Sun. Clouds form as the result of the condensation of rising hot air into the lower part of the atmosphere. Clear air descends to the ground where it is heated, then rises as it warms up; it goes up into the atmosphere where it cools and condensates, trapping a lot of water vapor, which in turn reflects the sunlight, making it less intense.

Global warming would evaporate more water and therefore more water vapor will go into the atmosphere and be trapped into clouds which will in turn cover more of the sky and decrease the intensity of sunlight that comes in. This could balance warming, but water vapor also traps infrared radiation.

LIFE

Why does life flourish on the Earth and not on any other planet? In this section we will take a look at the history of planetary evolution from the origin of life up to vertebrates and humans.

ORIGIN OF LIFE

In the early 1920s a young Russian biochemist, Aleksandr (Ivanovitch) Oparin, theorized that there must have been a beginning of life at a certain point in Earth's history and that we could make intelligent guesses as to when it was and how it occurred.

Oparin theorized that the atmosphere of the early Earth lacked oxygen but contained gases such as ammonia, methane and hydrogen. In that kind of atmosphere (without ozone), UV rays would have energized the components and generated the first synthetic reactions of organic compounds such as amino acids, the building block of life. These in turn would clump together in long chains and possibly take on the characteristics of the primitive cell. He called this early amalgamation of compounds **primordial soup**. Figure 17 diagrams this process.

Figure 17 Origin of Life

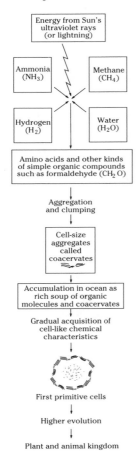

In the 1950s Stanley Miller devised an experiment that demonstrated how it may have happened. He built an apparatus that zapped a primordial soup with electrical jolts comparable to lightning, and produced amino acids. The step from amino acids to actual life and genetic coding is not yet understood. Other theories suggest that the early atmosphere was primarily carbon dioxide, water vapor and nitrogen, as expected from degassing of the Earth. In this environment, amino acids have also been produced.

Others propose that building blocks may have originated in nearby comets and come to Earth on impacts. The origin of the nucleic acids DNA and RNA that enable life to replicate and transmit genetic information to the offspring is not clear, but it is obvious that this was the final and most crucial step towards organized life.

If you ever watch the old "Star Trek" series, you may have seen a couple of episodes in which they discuss the possibility of life based on silicon instead of carbon (Si and C are of the same chemical group and possess many of the same characteristics). Silicon-based life is highly unlikely because one of the most outstanding properties of carbon is that it is gaseous at room temperature rather than solid like silicon. This property enabled carbon to make organic compounds in the fluid state, at low temperatures, with lower energy requirements than that of silicon. Silicon is too heavy and too inert to react at the temperatures at which life as we know it survives.

The first known organisms on Earth are some carbonaceous remains of primitive cells with no nucleus that date back 3.5 billion years. **Prokaryotes**, which still exist today in bacteria, algae, ameba, and other simple organisms, lack a nucleus, the central part that contains all the genetic material, as well as specialized organelles for other cellular activities. These first organisms were probably **anaerobic** and fed on methane.

EARLY ORGANISMS

Figure 18 Cell Types

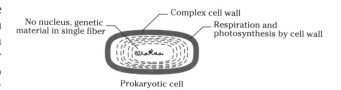

Prokaryotic cell

Two billion years ago, organized life—like algae—were thriving on the planet. One billion years ago the **eukaryotic** cell, the cell with a nucleus, developed. One of the most popular theories on the origin of eukaryotes is that two prokaryotic cells may have stayed together after mitosis (cell division) or they may have started a symbiotic relationship. One may have captured the other and from there the "trapped one" would have developed into a nucleus, and also into several different organelles that perform different activities, such as breathing, metabolizing, etc. inside the cell. This is seen in modern eukaryotes in that **mitochondria** (the organelles that breathe for us) have their own genetic material and replicate separately from the rest of the genetic material in the cell. Figure 18 shows the difference between eukaryotes and prokaryotes.

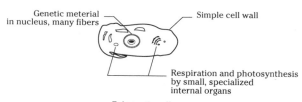

Eukaryotic cell

Shortly after the evolution of eukaryotic cells (in geologic time), the first multicellular organisms or **metazoans** evolved. With the advent of metazoans a very diverse range of life-forms evolved, including the development of soft-bodied organisms as seen in the Ediacara fauna of Australia and the Burgess shale in Canada.

Six hundred million years ago, after the explosion of diversity of soft-bodied organisms, the first shelled organisms developed in a period called the **Cambrian**.

The rate of evolution between one billion years ago and 600 million was so much higher than at earlier times that it could be termed explosive. From a world dominated by algae and bacteria we passed to a world full of different species that in some form or other still survive today. There were more species alive at that time than have evolved since.

The geologic time scales and the different life-forms at each period are shown in Table 4.

ERA	PERIOD	EVENTS	BEGAN MILLIONS OF YEARS AGO
CENOZOIC	Quateranary	Age of humans. Four major glacial advances.	2
	Tertiary	Increase in mammals. Appearance of primates. Mountain building in Europe and Asia.	65
MESOZOIC	Cretaceous	Extinction of dinosaurs. Increase in flowering plants and reptiles.	140
	Jurassic	Birds. Mammals. Dominance of dinosaurs. Mountain building in western North America.	195
	Triassic	Beginning of dinosaurs and primitive mammals.	230
PALEOZOIC	Permian	Reptiles spread and develop. Evaporate deposits. Glaciation in Southern Hemisphere.	280
	Carboniferous	Abundant amphibians. Reptiles appear.	345
	Devonian	Age of fishes. First amphibians. First abundant forests on land.	395
	Silurian	First land plants. Mountain building in Europe.	435
	Ordovician	First fishes and vertebrates.	500
	Cambrian	Age of marine invertebrates.	600
PRECAMBRIAN TIME		Beginning of life, at least five times longer than all geologic time following.	

Table 4

EVOLUTION OF OXYGEN-RICH ATMOSPHERE AND PHOTOSYNTHESIS

We have already stated that primitive life evolved in an anaerobic atmosphere with little or no oxygen. Obviously, many changes have occurred since. Even the Cambrian organisms needed oxygen to survive.

Around three billion years ago (with the advent of blue-green algae) organisms must have developed the ability to photosynthesize—take CO_2 from the atmosphere and with the aid of the sun's radiation, break it down and use the carbon to make the food, complex carbohydrates and other energy compounds that enabled the organism to survive. In return the organisms give free oxygen back to the atmosphere.

The oxygen must have started to accumulate in the atmosphere, and soon its levels would become high because few organisms were able to breathe and deplete it. The accumulation of oxygen was poisonous to many organisms, which must have died out as a consequence.

Some time just before 600 million years ago the amount of oxygen reached high enough levels to allow rapid evolution of the invertebrates in the Paleozoic period. For the rest of the life of the planet the amount of oxygen has been kept constant by photosynthetic organisms.

Life not only changed the atmosphere, but also changed the geology, by originating new types of sediments, rocks and geographical features such as coral reefs.

HISTORY AND DIVERSITY OF LIFE

Diversification of life had already taken place before the Cambrian explosion. That diversification is hard to describe because of a lack of fossil evidence, so we will concentrate on life from the Cambrian period on.

CAMBRIAN PERIOD— INVASION OF THE SEAS

The Cambrian initiation was the beginning of organisms with hard body parts or shells. This provided defense against predators and also prompted better fossil preservation. The most common hard body parts were made of calcite, chitin and SiO_2. The fossil record really begins at the beginning of the Cambrian era because of the better preservation of hard body parts.

The first fossils with hard skeletal parts were the **trilobites,** an extinct group of **arthropods** related to crabs, lobsters and shrimps. These first trilobites had large eyes, long antennae, and a well-developed nervous system. In the early Cambrian over 90% of all the fossils specimens were trilobites. Other common animals were the **brachiopods**, similar to clams, and some **echinoderms** (starfishes and sand dollars). Many other organisms became extinct and left no descendants. All these animals were marine and invaded the seas all around the world. Other marine organisms such as corals, mollusks, fish, etc., developed during the rest of the Paleozoic and also into the Mesozoic and Cenozoic.

INVASION OF LAND: PLANTS AND ANIMALS

The most outstanding achievement of the post-Cambrian Paleozoic was the invasion of land by the first plants and animals. This opened a lot of new **niches** (ecological habitats) for animals to evolve.

Organisms that lived underwater had gills or special systems to breathe, and in order to survive on land they needed to develop a vascular system that enabled them to use oxygen or carbon dioxide that was not dissolved in water. Plants did it first in the early Devonian period.

Transition from water to land took place in the Devonian and the mid-to-late Paleozoic periods. One of the reasons why it did not take place earlier is that there were extensive shallow seas over the land, so there was not very much dry land available.

Unfortunately the fossil record on land is not as good as the marine record because preservation is a lot worse on land. The record is spotty, discontinuous and full of gaps even in younger rocks.

PLANTS DO IT FIRST

In the mid-to-late Paleozoic plants developed a vascular system that allowed them to survive without being underwater. This system consisted of very narrow, elongated hollow cells through which water and food could circulate. It was also a way to maintain the needed water balance inside their bodies. They also needed to develop a rooting system (land plants need to be attached), and a support for the body like cellulose or lignin. Once these adaptations were developed, the first land plant could survive far away from water and depend only on precipitation and groundwater.

Further into the Paleozoic era, larger and more plants developed. The first land plants were small grass-like weeds or bushes. Later into the Carboniferous period, large ferns took over, and shortly after that came the conifers, which dominated most of the Mesozoic era. It was not until the end of the Mesozoic and the beginning of the Cenozoic that flowering plants, with their efficient reproductive system, came along.

LAND ANIMALS AND THE EVOLUTION TO HUMANS

In this section we will concentrate on the evolution of vertebrates after they reached the land, all the way to humans. We have not included a discussion on the mechanisms of evolution itself, although they will be mentioned in relation to theories of mass extinctions. We leave it to the reader to consult more specialized books on the subject.

The oldest known land animals including freshwater organisms were invertebrates or arthropods. A land scorpion and a millipede were found in early Devonian rocks. Insect-like fossils of this age have also been found. Snails and slugs do not appear until the late Paleozoic, after the tetrapods or four-legged vertebrates.

Apart from a few anomalous organisms, vertebrates evolved straight into fishes and from there into amphibians, reptiles, mammals and birds. Fishes will not be discussed except for their link to the invasion of land. Freshwater Devonian fishes, crossopterygians, had both lungs and gills for breathing, so they developed the most important adaptation for living on land: being able to breathe air and not water. They also had thick fleshy fins, which enabled them to walk. The fins gradually changed to short stubby legs. The bone structure of these fishes matches those of the early amphibians.

These adaptations, which undoubtedly were meant at first only to help them survive as successful freshwater fishes, then became useful to transfer completely to land. They were probably forced to transfer to land by changes in climate in the Devonian that dried up freshwater niches. There must have also been more food available on land as freshwater areas dried out.

After these fishes, the first real land animals in the fossil record are amphibians, the ancestors to toads and frogs. These animals lived on land near the water since they often had to go into the water to breathe and breed. As evolution proceeded the amphibians became better adapted to living on land by developing stronger limbs.

From one of the amphibian lineages the first reptiles evolved. Reptiles started appearing in the Carboniferous period and began dominating the environment up until the end of the Mesozoic era. The reptiles had a big advantage over the amphibians—they didn't need to go to the water to breed. Reptiles developed the amniotic egg, an egg with a hard, porous shell, which allowed the egg to survive without the constant presence of water for breathing. Unlike the amphibians, the reptile youngsters developed right from the egg without a larval or tadpole stage.

Several types of reptile lineages developed in the Paleozoic, but the two most important and interesting to us are the **Synapsida**, or mammal-like reptiles, from which mammals developed in the Mesozoic, and the **Diapsida**, or ruling reptiles, which included the dinosaurs. The end of the Paleozoic saw the development of many species of reptiles, especially the dinosaurs, which also proliferated, maybe even more, throughout the Mesozoic. There were many kinds of dinosaurs: herbivores, carnivores, flying, aquatic, etc.

Mammal-like reptiles developed in the Triassic (the beginning of the Mesozoic). These reptiles had longer and stronger limbs than the other reptiles and their brain cases became progressively larger. Their dental structure approached that of modern mammals.

The ruling reptiles had one important group, the **thecodonts**, which then became the dinosaurs. These animals were bipedal and had tiny skulls. The front limbs were not used for walking but for handling food. Two main groups of dinosaurs became important: those with a pelvic bone similar to other reptiles (saurischians) and those with a pelvic girdle similar to birds (ornitischians). Saurischians were small and from them developed the large predators of the late Mesozoic such as Tyrannosaurus rex. Most dinosaurs nonetheless were herbivores, not carnivores.

From dinosaurs developed the first bird-like reptiles, and from them, birds. A very famous bird-like reptile is Archaeopteryx, which had feathers and a wing structure very similar to modern-day birds.

As mentioned before, mammals evolved from the Synapsida, the mammal-like reptiles. The first mammals were small, with small brain capacity; most of them were probably rodents (mice, etc.). Mammals were not very common in the Mesozoic, except for rodents and monotremes (duck-bill platypus). Not until after the demise of the dinosaurs at the end of the Cretaceous did they start taking over the land, especially with the evolution of **placental** and **marsupial** mammals.

Marsupials (kangaroos and opossums, for example) are animals that give birth to young incapable of fending for themselves; the mother keeps them in a pouch outside her body until they are fit for life on their own. Many types of marsupials are only found in Australia and New Zealand. This is because early during their speciation the continents separated (the breakup of Pangaea), isolating Australia from the rest of the world.

Placentals give birth to completely developed offspring that feed from the milk produced by the mother's mammary glands. After a short period of milking they are ready to start life on their own.

Mammals are very familiar to us: rodents, canines and felines (dogs and cats), ruminants (cows), and others. Those most important in human evolution are the primates.

Primates originated in the Early Tertiary period, after the demise of the dinosaurs. They were omnivores rather than insectivores. They adapted to life in trees—one of their fundamental evolutionary steps was the development of a grasping hand with an opposable thumb. Another adaptation was the forward migration of the eyes, which provides stereoscopic or three-dimensional vision.

Primates known to us are the **simians** (monkeys) and **anthropoideans** (man-like).

Simians were preceded by prosimians, which gave rise to the true monkeys and apes of the simians. In the anthropoideans there are three groups: New World monkeys, Old World monkeys and Hominoids, which includes human beings and apes. The only one we will talk about in some detail is the Hominoids.

HOMINOIDS AND HUMAN EVOLUTION

The hominoids include the chimpanzee, the orangutan, the gorilla, the gibbon and human beings. It isn't until the Oligocene (~35–24 million years ago) that these groups start differentiating. Of all these groups, one genus dating back to the late Miocene (~5 million years ago) is apparently the direct ancestor to modern human beings. This is the so-called **Ramapithecus**. Homo sapiens developed in the Pleistocene about 4 million years ago during the glaciation epochs. The upright posture and ground-dwelling habits of human beings were already established in Ramapithecus. This is also true of other apes. Grasping hands are common to all primates and the use of tools is observed in chimpanzees. Language has been taught to chimpanzees and gorillas, although their vocal chords are different than ours. They can also teach it to their offspring as proven in some recent experiments.

What makes human beings strikingly different than the rest of the primates is their brain capacity—much larger with respect to their size than any other primate. The development of a complete, complex language is also a characteristic of human beings.

Human beings are the only animals that are capable of totally modifying their environment, for better or for worse. They are the only animal capable of creating new niches and modifying existing ones.

Another characteristic that distinguishes a human being from an animal is the ability to think of the long-term future. Human beings and animals share the memory of the past and the living in the present, but human beings are unique in predicting the future and also in questioning their existence.

The evolution of early human beings is shown in Figure 19. There are three principal stages in the evolution of early human beings: Australopithecus, Homo erectus, and Homo sapiens. The first stage is the one to which the famous Lucy, discovered by Donald Johannsen, belongs. The Australopithecines were similar to modern human beings, but although they used tools and weapons, they

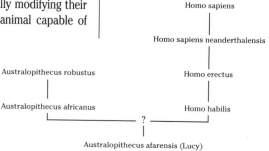

Australopithecus afarensis (Lucy) - found only in Africa; walked before the development of a large brain (compared to ours).

Homo habilis - first tool maker.

Homo erectus - made achellian (core) tools; migrated out of Africa.

Homo sapiens - made blade tools (flaking); also migrated out of Africa; development of agriculture, etc.

Figure 19 The Human Evolutionary Lineage

had very small brains. Homo erectus lived at the same time as the Australopithecines, and may have developed independently. The species was more advanced than the Australopithecines and had a higher brain capacity. They used stone tools, such as hand axes, made from flint. This species became widely distributed and is the direct ancestor of modern human beings.

Fossils of Homo erectus range in age from 700,000 to 200,000 years old. Homo sapiens is contemporaneous in age with Homo erectus, appearing for the first time 500,000 years ago. The first example of sapiens is Neanderthal Man, a large-boned race that lived 100,000 years ago. After sapiens originated, different historical ages developed, such as the Paleolithic and Neolithic.

FOOD CHAINS

A subject of great importance in a world with an ever-growing population is the availability of food. The food chain is an organizational scheme that describes which organisms feed on which, and which ones are essential for the survival of the others. It is like a pyramid because the organisms at the base are most abundant.

At the base of our food chain are organisms that produce their own food: photosynthetic organisms such as bacteria, plants, and plankton in the oceans. Upon these feed higher organisms, herbivores (plant-eaters) and omnivores (eating both animal and vegetable matter). If the plants were to die, all cows will die as a consequence—there would be no food left for them.

On top of herbivores at the peak of the food chain are carnivores (animal-eaters) and omnivores. Good examples are lions, tigers, cats, dogs and humans.

If we kill photosynthetic organisms by deforestation, polluting the oceans or by other environmental problems, we affect the base of the food chain and decrease the possibility of survival of the top of the chain—including ourselves.

MASS EXTINCTIONS

Mass extinctions are very important events that affect the rates at which evolution occurs. A mass extinction is defined as the death of 70% or more of the total biomass of the planet at any given time. Biomass is the total weight of all living matter on the planet. Mass extinctions have occurred at least five times in the geologic past within the **Phanerozoic** alone. Extinctions during and before the Cambrian are difficult to document.

The most massive extinction known occurred 225 million years ago at the Permian-Triassic boundary. Another one occurred at the next boundary, Triassic-Jurassic, about 190 million years ago. During the Cretaceous another important extinction occurred around 100 million years ago.

The second largest extinction was at the Cretaceous-Tertiary boundary, when all the dinosaurs became extinct. The mass extinction of the dinosaurs has become very famous partially due to the hypothesis that the cause of the extinction was an extraterrestrial object: a meteorite.

Mass extinctions are important because even though a large sector of the population was wiped out, niches were left available for newcomers that could adapt very fast and evolve rapidly into many new species. This seems to be the case after every extinction—a new group of living organisms takes over and evolves at a very high rate. During periods of time without mass extinctions, species also become extinct, but at a low rate, an event known as a **background extinction**. Evolution also takes place very slowly during such periods.

Are mass extinctions catastrophic or are they gradual events? The debate continues. It was generally believed that mass extinctions were a slow, gradual process like evolution but more and more evidence is being uncovered concerning the sudden disappearance of many unrelated species at the same time. This has been proven at the Cretaceous-Tertiary boundary, where within one centimeter of rock (which corresponds to a relatively short period of time) all evidence of Cretaceous fossils disappears and Tertiary fossils come into play. This kind of boundary impact layer can be seen in Gubbio, Italy.

NEMESIS AND THE IMPACT THEORY

We have mentioned the extinction 65 million years ago at the Cretaceous-Tertiary boundary of dinosaurs. Dinosaurs were not the only animals that died: **ammonites**, very important marine fossils, also went extinct, as well as many other land and marine animals and plants.

One of the marine groups that went extinct is the planktic forams (small, calcareous, floating unicellular organisms that lived in Cretaceous seas). These organisms are found in limestones in the Apennines of Italy. The last bed of the Cretaceous limestone has big planktic forams; the first bed of the Tertiary has one small planktic foram and nothing else. In between is a layer of clay about 3 cm thick known as the "boundary clay."

In 1980, Luis and Walter Alvarez from UC Berkeley took samples of that clay to measure the amount of an element called **iridium**, which is not very abundant on the Earth's surface but more abundant in extraterrestrial objects. Iridium rains at a constant rate, which made it very useful for measuring the amount of

time it took to deposit the layer of clay and therefore how long it took for the extinction to happen. When they measured the samples of boundary clay, they found that the levels were low in the limestone above and below the clay, but within the clay, iridium was at a high peak—at the same level as that in meteorites and comets.

They hypothesized that the extra iridium was from extraterrestrial sources, and that at the time of the Cretaceous-Tertiary extinction there had been a large meteorite (10 km in diameter) that had hit the Earth. The dust from the impact would have gone into the atmosphere, causing total darkness for several months, inhibiting photosynthesis and cutting the food chain at the base. Other effects of the impact would have been extreme cold, heat and also acid rain. Other evidence for impact, such as shocked minerals, was found in Italy and in another 100 sites around the world, which made plausible the global mass extinctions.

Against this hypothesis is the fact that the crater of the impact has not been found, which may mean that it occurred in the ocean and that part of the ocean has been subducted—it has moved underneath a ridge in plate tectonic activity.

This hypothesis led to findings of many impact craters and also of other boundaries associated with iridium anomalies. It also generated interest in extinctions that seemed to repeat themselves periodically.

A study by two paleontologists from Chicago showed that there was a certain cyclicity to extinctions occurring every 26–28 million years. This led Rich Muller, an astrophysicist at U.C. Berkeley, to hypothesize that the Sun has a companion star, Nemesis, which orbits around the Sun in a tulip orbit with a period of 26–28 million years and that at its perihelion it disturbed a belt of comets and asteroids outside the Solar System. This sent comets and asteroids into the inner Solar System and caused periodic comet showers on the Earth, and as a consequence, periodic extinctions.

The original statistical data showing periodicity in mass extinctions were sketchy and poorly constrained. To base Nemesis on it was an exercise in creativity—the search for Nemesis has so far been unsuccessful.

VOLCANISM

For many a geologist, accepting a catastrophic extraterrestrial event has been difficult, so, two Earth scientists from Dartmouth University proposed that the extra iridium came from big volcanic eruptions occurring at the same time as the extinctions. This was hypothesized because iridium was found in the gases emitted by Kilauea. A candidate for the big volcanic event that would have sent the iridium and dust in the atmosphere to stop photosynthesis and kill the dinosaurs would be the Deccan Traps of India, a big basaltic eruption dated at 66 million years. However, no evidence of iridium has been found in the Deccan Traps, and the type of volcanic eruption of these basalts was quiet and not violent enough to send material into the stratosphere to orbit around the Earth (as required by the global distribution of iridium). It also would not produce impact minerals, although some scientists claim it does (no evidence has been uncovered as to this effect). Volcanism may have had something to do with local extinctions, but not at a global level.

GLACIATIONS

Finally, many argue that climatic fluctuations and changes in sea level could have caused sudden extinctions. Although there are data to support contemporaneous extinctions and climatic changes, it is hard to see how gradual changes in the climate, changes in sea level and slow glaciation, and interglaciation periods could have caused sudden mass extinction of all types of animals, even those used to living in cold climates.

SimEarth

HUMAN CIVILIZATIONS AND TECHNOLOGY

The developments—and disintegrations—of civilizations span thousands of years, encompassing spectacular advances in knowledge and sharply disruptive disturbances on the human and planetary scale. This section will encapsulate the development of human endeavor from the Paleolithic to the Atomic Ages, outlining the technological movements that have accompanied and spurred the advance of culture.

Civilization is generally regarded as culture with a relatively high degree of elaboration and technical development, often demarcated by the complex of cultural elements that first appeared in human history 6,000 to 8,000 years ago. At that time, on the basis of agriculture, stock-raising and metallurgy, intensive occupational specialization began to appear in the river valleys of SW Asia. However, the roots of those circumstances long predate that period in several parts of the prehistoric world: Mesopotamia, Egypt, China, Greece, India, Highland Peru, and elsewhere.

THE OLD STONE AGE (PALEOLITHIC)

The specific characteristics of civilization—food production, plant and animal domestication, metallurgy, a high degree of occupational specialization, writing and the growth of cities—had their origins in the the Old Stone Age, the earliest period of human development and the longest phase of humanity's history.

The Old Stone Age is approximately coextensive with the Pleistocene geologic period, beginning about two million years ago and ending in various places between 40,000 and 10,000 years ago, when it was succeeded by the Mesolithic Period.

By far the most outstanding feature of the Paleolithic period was the evolution of humans from an apelike creature, or near human, to true Homo sapiens. This development was exceedingly slow and continued through the three successive divisions of the period, the Lower, Middle and Upper Paleolithic.

The most abundant remains of Paleolithic cultures are a variety of stone tools whose distinct characteristics provide the basis for a system of classification containing several toolmaking traditions or industries. The oldest recognizable tools made by members of the family of humankind are simple stone choppers, such as those discovered at Olduvai Gorge in Tanzania. These tools may have been made over one million years ago by Australopithecus or by Homo habilis. Fractured stone "tools" called **eoliths** have been considered the earliest tools, but it has been difficult to distinguish human-made from naturally produced modifications in such stones.

THE LOWER PALEOLITHIC

Lower Paleolithic stone industries of Homo erectus have been found at various sites in China, Europe, Africa and Asia dating from 100,000 to 500,000 years ago. The stone tools of this period are of the core type, made by chipping the stone to form a cutting edge, or of the flake type, fashioned from fragments struck off a stone. Hand axes were the typical tool of these early people, who were hunters and food gatherers.

THE MIDDLE PALEOLITHIC

The Middle Paleolithic period is often associated with Neanderthals, living between 40,000 and 100,000 years ago. Neanderthal remains are often found in caves with evidence of the use of fire. Neanderthals were hunters of prehistoric mammals and their cultural remains, though unearthed chiefly in Europe, have also been found in N Africa, Palestine and Siberia.

Stone tools of this period are of the flake tradition, and bone implements, such as needles, indicate that crudely sewn furs and skins were used as body covering.

THE UPPER PALEOLITHIC

The Upper Paleolithic saw the disappearance of Neanderthal in favor of other Homo sapiens such as Cro-Magnon. The beginnings of communal hunting and fishing are found here, as is the first conclusive evidence of belief systems centering on magic and the supernatural. Pit houses, the first human-made shelters were built, sewn clothing was worn, and sculpture and painting originated. Tools were of great variety, including flint and obsidian blades and projectile points.

The final and perhaps most impressive phase of the Paleolithic period is the Magdalenian period, in which communities of fisherman and reindeer hunters used highly refined and varied tools and weapons, and left an impressive array of cave paintings.

THE MESOLITHIC PERIOD

This period began with the end of the last glacial period and involved the gradual domestication of plants and animals and the formation of settled communities at various times and places, some overlapping into the considerable development of the Neolithic period.

Characteristic of the period were hunting and fishing settlements along rivers and on lake shores. Pottery and the use of the bow began to develop. Hafted axes and bone tools were found in the Baltic region and N England, demonstrating strong advances over Paleolithic crudity.

The Mesolithic period in several areas shows a gradual transition from a food-collecting to a food-producing culture.

THE NEOLITHIC REVOLUTION

Toward the end of that last ice age, some 15,000 to 20,000 years ago, a few of the human communities that were most favored by geography and climate began to make the transition from the long period of Paleolithic savagery to a more settled way of life depending on animal husbandry and agriculture.

This period of transition led to a marked rise in population, to a growth in the size of communities, and to the beginnings of town life. It is sometimes referred to as the Neolithic Revolution because the speed of technological innovation increased so greatly and the social and political organization of human groups underwent a corresponding increase in complexity.

The earliest known development of Neolithic culture was in SW Asia between 8000 B.C. and 6000 B.C. Settled villages cultivating wheat, barley and millet and raising cattle, sheep, goats and pigs expanded. Neolithic culture and its innovations spread through Europe, the Nile valley, the Indus valley (India) and the Yellow River valley (China).

By 1500 B.C., Neolithic cultures based on the cultivation of maize, beans, squash and other plants were present in Mexico and South America, leading to the rise of the Inca and Aztec civilizations and spreading to other parts of the Americas by the time of European contact.

THE BRONZE AGE

This is the period in the development of technology when metals were first used regularly in the manufacture of tools and weapons. Pure copper and bronze, an alloy of copper and tin, were used indiscriminately at first; this early period is sometimes called the Copper Age.

The earliest use of cast metal can be deduced from clay models of weapons; casting was certainly established in the Middle East by 3500 B.C. In the New World, the earliest bronze was cast in Bolivia A.D. c.1100. The Inca civilization used bronze tools and weapons but never mastered iron.

The development of a metallurgical industry coincided with the rise of urbanization. The organized operations of mining, smelting, and casting undoubtedly required the specialization of labor and the production of surplus food to support a class of artisans, while the search for raw materials stimulated the exploration and colonization of new territories.

THE IRON AGE

This period begins with the general use of iron and continues into modern times. The use of smelted iron ornaments and ceremonial weapons became common during the period extending from 1900 to 1400 B.C. About this time, the invention of tempering, the strengthening of a metal by the application of heat or by alternate heating and cooling, was made in the Hittite empire. After its downfall in 1200 B.C., the great waves of migrants spreading through S Europe and the Middle East ensured the rapid transmission of iron technology.

The casting of iron did not become technically useful until the Industrial Revolution. The people of the Iron Age developed the basic economic innovations of the Bronze Age and laid the foundations for feudal organization. Ox-drawn plows and wheeled vehicles acquired a new importance and changed the agricultural patterns. For the first time humans were able to exploit efficiently the temperate forest. Villages were fortified, warfare was conducted on horseback and in horse-drawn chariots, and alphabetic writing based on the Phoenician script became widespread.

CLASHES, CONQUESTS, AND CHANGE

Technical advances in weaponry and warfare helped an insignificant pastoral settlement in Rome to become perhaps the world's most successful empire—supreme as a lawgiver and organizer, holding sway over virtually all the then-known world.

From the establishment of the Roman republic around 500 B.C. successive generations of Roman rulers expanded their territorial acquisitions, and thus absorbed and exported the leading material, social and intellectual advances of the day.

From the age of Caesar, (60 B.C.) Rome was foremost as the civilizer of barbarians and the ruler of the older world. The empire promulgated the ideals of Greek literature, architecture and thought. The extensive system of Roman roads made transportation easier than it was again to be until the development of railroads. A postal service was organized; commerce and industry, particularly by sea, were greatly developed.

At its height, imperial Rome counted well over one million inhabitants. It was well-policed, sanitation was excellent, and among the rich, such luxuries as central heating and running water were not unknown. Decline came quickly, however. In 476 the last emperor of the West, appropriately called Romulus Augustus, was deposed by the Goths; this date is commonly accepted as the end of the West Roman Empire, or Western Empire.

The so-called Dark Ages that followed in Western Europe could not eradicate the profound imprint left by Roman civilization.

THE INDUSTRIAL REVOLUTION

This term is usually applied to the social and economic changes that marked the transition from a stable agricultural and commercial society to a modern industrial society relying on complex machinery rather than tools. Historically, it refers primarily to the period in British history from the middle of the 18th century to the middle of the 19th century. Dramatic changes in the social and economic structure took place: inventions and technological innovations created the factory system of large-scale machine production, greater economic specialization emerged and the laboring population, formerly employed predominantly in agriculture (where production was also on the rise), increasingly gathered in great urban factory centers. The same process occurred at later times and in changed tempo in other countries.

There has been much objection to the term because the word "revolution" suggests sudden, violent, unparalleled change, whereas the transformation was, to a great extent, gradual. Some historians argue that the 13th and 16th centuries were also periods of revolutionary economic change. The ground was prepared by the voyages of discovery from Western Europe in the 15th and 16th centuries, which led to a vast influx of precious metals from the New World, raising prices, stimulating industry, and fostering a money economy. Expansion of trade and the money economy stimulated the development of new institutions of finance and credit.

In Britain's productive process, coal came to replace wood. Early model steam engines were introduced to drain water and raise coal from the mines. Factories and industrial towns sprang up. Canals and roads were built, and the advent of the railroad and the steamship widened the market for manufactured goods. The Bessemer Process made a gigantic contribution, for it was largely responsible for the extension of the use of steam and steel that were the two chief features of industry in the middle of the 19th century. The transformation of the United States into an industrial nation took place largely after the Civil War and on the British model. The Industrial Revolution was introduced by Europeans into Asia, and the last years of the 19th and the early 20th century saw the development of industries in India, China and Japan.

The Industrial Revolution created a specialized and interdependent economic life and made urban workers more completely dependent on the will of their employers than the rural workers had been. Relations between capital and labor were aggravated, and Marxism was one product of this unrest.

The Industrial Revolution changed the face of nations, giving rise to urban centers requiring vast municipal services. Technology was praised by some factions as the mainspring of social progress and the development of democracy, and criticized by others as the bane of modern man, responsible for the tyranny of the machine and the squalor of urban life.

Machines had vastly increased production, eased the toils of labor and raised living standards, but often at a cost of environmental pollution, depletion of natural resources, and the creation of unsatisfying jobs.

THE ATOMIC AGE

With the advent of the Atomic Age we must face the contemporary dilemma of a highly technological society contemplating the possibility that it could use its sophisticated techniques in order to accomplish its own destruction. It is not a firm assumption to identify technology with the "progressive" forces in contemporary civilization. The forces of technology will continue their seemingly inexorable advance, bringing us in vitro fertilizations, global satellite communications, genetic manipulations and B2 bombers, but the wisdom to manage these innovations is not a guaranteed part of the package.

SimEarth

THEORIES OF THE EARTH: THE GAIA HYPOTHESIS

SimEarth is centered around a hypothesis of the evolution of the Earth, life and atmosphere known as the **Gaia hypothesis**, proposed by James Lovelock. The Gaia hypothesis is a holistic approach to understanding life and natural phenomena as teleological circumstances, that is, as existing because they fill a purpose and not just because of happenstance. Here is a brief explanation of what the Gaia hypothesis is and a few of the examples given by Lovelock.

SYSTEMS

Figure 20 Positive and Negative Feedback Loops

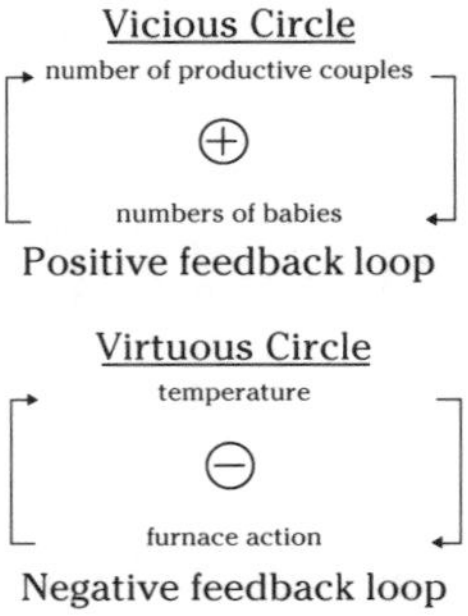

Vicious Circle

number of productive couples

$\oplus$

numbers of babies

Positive feedback loop

Virtuous Circle

temperature

$\ominus$

furnace action

Negative feedback loop

Before we start talking about Gaia we need to define what the feedback mechanisms "positive" and "negative" mean. A positive feedback loop is also known in systems theory as a vicious circle or catastrophic loop. As illustrated in Figure 20, a positive loop is the one that causes continuous increase or decrease of a certain condition resulting in a catastrophe. A negative feedback loop is a self-regulating feedback loop or virtuous circle: a mechanism like a thermostat, where if a certain condition increases, the next decreases, resulting in equilibrium or self-regulation.

Most of Earth's systems, like the carbon cycle and the atmospheric hydrologic cycle, are self-regulatory and tend toward equilibrium. Nonetheless, most systems can be driven over the edge and would never be able to self-regulate again if a certain critical threshold of one of the conditions is reached. This could happen with atmospheric CO_2.

GAIA

The Gaia hypothesis comes in two versions: the weak Gaia and the strong Gaia. The strong Gaia says that the Earth is alive. The weak Gaia says that life may have some regulatory effect on some of the dynamic systems of the planet. We will explore in this manual only the strong Gaia version. Please understand that although this hypothesis is controversial and therefore not generally accepted in the scientific community, it provides a useful framework for understanding the Earth.

Gaia was developed by Lovelock during the time NASA was preparing the Viking explorer for a trip to Mars. He was designing instrumentation to test if there was life there. But in order to test for life, Lovelock had to ask the question, "What is life?" This work provided Lovelock the opportunity to reevaluate this fundamental question.

Page 196   *An Introduction to Earth Science*

Lovelock realized that we needn't go to Mars to find out if there was life, because if there were, we would see changes reflected in its atmospheric composition and other planetary features like those we see on the Earth, which has a very peculiar atmosphere. Life as we know it would affect the planet's atmosphere, as shown in Table 5.

GAS	VENUS	EARTH (without life)	MARS	EARTH
CO_2 (%)	96.5	98	95	0.03
N_2 (%)	3.5	1.9	2.7	79
O_2 (%)	trace	0.0	0.13	21
Ar	70. ppm	0.1	1.6	1
Methane	0.0	0.0	0.0	1.7 ppm
Surf. Temp.	459° C	240-340° C	-53° C	13° C
Total Pressure	90 bars	60 bars	.0064 bars	1.0 bars

Table 5 Origin of Atmospheric Composition

DAISYWORLD

Lovelock invented a very simple world model called Daisyworld to explain the tenets of the Gaia hypothesis. The parable of Daisyworld begins by explaining that it is a fictitious planet in which the life is represented by different-colored daisies: dark, light and neutral colors.

The planet is at the same distance from the Sun as the Earth, is the same size as the Earth and has a little more land area than the Earth. On this planet there is enough CO_2 for daisies, but it does not affect the climate like on the Earth and clouds do not exist.

The Sun increases its heat output with age. The optimum temperature for daisies is about 20° C. If the planet gets colder than 5° C, daisies will not grow. If it gets hotter than 40° C, they will die.

The average temperature of the planet is determined by the albedo, which is determined by the color of the daisies. A dark daisy absorbs more heat and the temperature rises; a lighter daisy reflects more heat and the temperature falls. This effect will make white and dark daisies alternate in population size until they eventually reach equilibrium, a condition in which all acting influences are cancelled by others resulting in a stable, balanced, or unchanging system. The

effect will also control the temperature of the planet. When the Sun gets hotter the temperature cannot be regulated anymore by the daisies and they die—the planet becomes barren.

The Daisyworld model illustrates the following tenets of the Gaia theory:

1. Living organisms grow vigorously, exploiting any environmental opportunities that open
2. Organisms are subject to the rules of Darwinian natural selection
3. Organisms affect their physical and chemical environment, by breathing, for example
4. Limits of constraints and bounds establish the limits of life

A version of the Daisyworld program is included as one of the SimEarth scenarios. There is a complete discussion of how and why Daisyworld works in the "Scenarios" chapter.

EVIDENCE OF REGULATION BY LIFE

Lovelock's book, *The Ages of Gaia*, examines the pollution of the atmosphere by oxygen producers and its consequences.

Many nations are extremely concerned about global warming, but it is not clearly understood how the Earth regulates the amount of CO_2 in the atmosphere. From the very beginning of life, CO_2 has been important in providing food for photosynthesizers, and as the thermal cover to keep us warm. Biota (life) pumps CO_2 from the atmosphere; its level has been going down for the last 3.6 billion years.

The increase in CO_2 due to the burning of fossil fuels is not much more than a minor disturbance to the Earth, but tends to offset the decline. Even though the quantities humans add may be small, if the CO_2 regulatory mechanism is reaching its capacity, then the plants that evolved as the CO_2 levels declined through Earth's history may be affected. Also, the rapid rise of CO_2 levels since the Industrial Revolution may indicate that the regulatory pumps are not working properly to remove the excessive CO_2 from the atmosphere.

This change in CO_2 is similar to the one that occurred naturally from the last ice age, so it may affect the climate as much as between the last ice age and now. We do not know enough about the CO_2 system to predict if the perturbation will self-regulate, cause oscillations, chaotic changes or total failure.

The possible climactic changes due to the increase in CO_2 probably won't have tragic consequences for the Earth and life as a whole, but it may wipe out humanity along with many other species of plants and animals.

GEOLOGY

1. Francis, Peter, 1976, **Volcanoes**, Penguin Books, England
2. Press, F. and Siever, R., 1986, **Earth**, fourth edition, Freeman, New York
3. Skinner, B.J., and Porter, S.C., 1989, **The Dynamic Earth**, J. Wiley and Sons, New York
4. Uyeda, S., 1978, **The New View of the Earth**, Freeman, New York

CLIMATE

1. Iribarne, J.V., and Cho, H., 1980, **Atmospheric Physics**, Reidel Publishing Co., Holland
2. Neiburger, M., Edinger, J.G., and Bonner, W.D., 1982, **Understanding Our Atmospheric Environment**, Freeman, New York
3. Riehl, H., 1978, **Introduction to the Atmosphere**, McGraw-Hill, New York
4 Ross, D., 1988, **Introduction to Oceanography**, Prentice-Hall, New Jersey

LIFE

1. Lane, G., 1978, **Life of the Past**, Charles Merrill Publishing Co., London
2. McAlester, A.L., 1977, **The History of Life**, Prentice-Hall, New Jersey
3. Muller, R., 1988, **Nemesis, the Death Star**, Weidenfeld and Nicolson, New York

GAIA

1. Lovelock, J., 1988, **The Ages of Gaia**, Norton, New York
2. Myers, Norman, 1984, **Gaia, an Atlas of Planet Management,** Anchor Press, New York

YET ANOTHER BLANK PAGE

APPENDICES

"The greatest planets
of mice and men oft go
extinct."

PROBLEMS AND SOLUTIONS

Here is a listing of common problems and challenges you will face, their causes, and some suggestions on how to deal with them.

PLANET OVERHEATING

First, check CO_2 levels. If high, use Oxygenator, or increase Biomes to reduce CO_2 levels.

You can also turn down solar input, raise cloud albedo, and turn down greenhouse effect.

EVOLUTION IN THE WATER SEEMS TO STOP

Most advanced aquatic life forms live in shallow water. If there are not enough shallow shelves, you will hit an evolutionary dead-end. You can create shelves either by raising the ocean floor or lowering the land. You can raise the ocean floor with the SET ALTITUDE tool or with volcanos. You can lower the land with the SET ALTITUDE tool or with meteors.

"... NEEDS ENERGY"

If you see a message that says that one of the disciplines (Philosophy, Science, Agriculture, Medicine, Art/Media) needs energy, increase their share of energy in the CIVILIZATION MODEL CONTROL PANEL, or increase the overall level of energy.

Overall energy is increased by doing more work, by increasing population, and by concentrating on the most efficient energy sources.

METEOR STORM

This is a warning that extinctions are imminent. There's not much to be done except prepare for the worst and get ready to rebuild your biomass.

MASS EXTINCTIONS

Mass Extinctions are caused by too much dust or too little oxygen (<20%) in the atmosphere.

Dust is put into the atmosphere by volcanos and meteor impacts. Nothing but time removes dust from the atmosphere.

If oxygen levels are below 20%, use the Oxygenator terraforming tool, or increase biomes.

FUELS RUNNING LOW

This is a warning that war is imminent. Change your energy usage to conserve fuels.

NUCLEAR DETONATIONS

Nuclear war is in progress. In SimEarth, this is caused by competition for limited nuclear fuels. Reduce investment in nuclear energy to halt the wars.

NUCLEAR WINTER

Caused by the radiation and dust in the air that result from numerous nuclear explosions. Cut back on fuel usage, and concentrate on keeping small pockets of your sentient species alive. Eventually the dust will settle and the radiation zones will vanish. Tidal waves can help clean up radiation in the oceans and on the shores.

POLLUTION

Pollution comes from industrial age technologies, as well as fossil fuel usage. The best solution is to invest in science and advance to the atomic era as quickly as possible.

SimEarth

GLOSSARY

Aerobic — Requires oxygen. This can apply to animals, machines or processes.

Air Pressure — The pressure caused by air molecules bouncing against a surface. Vacuum has no air pressure.

Albedo — The reflectivity of a surface. A surface with high albedo will reflect sunlight. A surface with low albedo will absorb sunlight. Snow (high albedo) reflects sunlight and remains cold.

Anaerobic — Does not require oxygen. This can apply to animals, machines or processes.

Arctic — Areas that are snow or ice covered. Cold and dry. See Tundra.

Arthropod — The phylum of animals which includes insects, crustaceans, arachnids, and myriapods.

Atmosphere — The blanket of gases which envelop a planet.

Atomic Age — This era is characterized by Nuclear Power, Aircraft, Radio, and Chemical Fertilizers.

Axis — The planetary center of rotation. On Earth, the axis is a line passing from the north pole to the south pole.

Biomass — The total dry weight of all living material on a planet.

Biome — A major ecosystem such as temperate grassland, forest or desert.

Biome Factory — A SimEarth tool which produces the best biome for the environment it occupies.

Biosphere — The areas of a planet which are inhabited by life. On Earth this is the crust, hydrosphere, and lower atmosphere.

Boreal — Also known as Boreal Forest. Biome designed for cool regions with airborn moisture. The trees are usually conifers.

Bronze — An alloy of tin and copper that is stronger than either.

Bronze Age — This era is characterized by bronze tools, sail ships, clay tablets and irrigation.

Carbon Dioxide (CO_2) — A gas composed of two oxygen atoms and one carbon atom. This gas is used by plants in photosynthesis and produced by organisms as they respirate.

Carniferns — A SimEarth name for mobile, carnivorous plants. The Venus Flytrap is the precursor to carniferns.

Cetaceans — The order of mammals that is exclusively aquatic. This includes dolphins and whales.

CO_2 Generator — A SimEarth tool that creates carbon dioxide for the atmosphere.

Class — The classification of life under Phylum. The major classes of Chordata are fish, amphibian, reptile, avian, and mammal. See Order.

Cloud Albedo — The albedo of clouds. High cloud albedo can keep Earth cool. See Albedo.

Conifer — Cone-bearing trees and shrubs. This includes evergreens, pines and firs.

Continental Drift — The theory that continents have changed position on Earth. This is a component of Plate Tectonics.

Core — The extremely dense, fluid center of Earth. It is probably composed of molten iron. See Mantle.

Crust — This thin outer shell of the Earth is only a few miles deep. See Mantle.

Cryosphere — The frozen regions such as the icecaps, tundra, and mountain glaciers.

Desert — An ecosystem suited for hot weather and little water.

Dry Weight — The mass of an organism after the water has been removed.

Dust — In SimEarth, dust refers to airborne dust, ash and detritus. This can darken a planet, reducing photosynthesis and absorbing heat.

Ecosystem — A group of plant and animal species living together in rough balance.

Eukaryote — Single-cell microbes with a nucleus.

Evolution — The process by which life has changed and diversified.

Explosive Upwelling — Sometimes hot spots are very hot. This can lead to a volcano that is a thousand times the size of any seen by man. These upwellings spew the material for continents and are possibly Nemesis.

Extinction — The elimination of one species.

Geosphere — See Lithosphere.

Greenhouse Effect — Planetary heating induced by greenhouse gases.

Greenhouse Gases — Certain gases will let solar radiation enter the atmosphere but not leave. The most common of these are carbon dioxide, methane, and water vapor.

Hot Spot — Mantle material flows up and down as well as sideways. Hot magma sometimes rises from the core to the crust creating a Hot Spot. See Volcano.

Hydrosphere — The water portions of Earth. This includes oceans, lakes, rivers, and clouds. SimEarth restricts the term to oceans.

Industrial Age — This era is characterized by the use of fossil-fuel engines, automobiles, telephones, and animal husbandry.

Information Age — This era is characterized by computers, global communications, robotic labor, and ecologic awareness.

Insolation — INcoming SOLar radiATION.

Iron Age — This era is characterized by iron tools, sextants, paper, the printing press, and horse-drawn plows.

Kingdom — The most general classification of life in Biology. The five kingdoms are prokaryotae, protoctista (eukaryotes), fungi, plantae and animalia.

Jungle (Tropical Forest) — A biome that thrives in hot, wet climates.

Lava — The lighter materials of magma that come to the surface via volcanos and upwellings.

Lithosphere — The rock portions of the planet: Plates, Crust, Moho, Mantle, and Core.

Magma — Molten rock found beneath the Earth's crust. See Lava.

Mantle — The layer of magma between the crust and core of the Earth. This area is constantly flowing at a speed measured in centimeters per year.

Mass Extinctions — At various times in Earth's history large numbers of species have vanished. Records indicate that at each of these times between 5% and 50% of the species became extinct. See Nemesis.

Methane (CH_4) — A gas composed of one carbon atom and four hydrogen atoms. It is primarily produced by primitive microbes which currently live in the intestines of larger organisms.

Microbe — A single-celled organism.

Mollusk — Class of invertebrates that includes snails, mussels and octopus.

Monolith — A SimEarth tool for advancing life. Thank you Arthur C. Clark.

Moho — Also called the Mohorovicic discontinuity. The turbulent region between the crust and the mantle.

Mutate — When an organism makes an inexact copy of itself. The variability which allows evolution to occur.

N_2 Generator — A SimEarth tool for introducing Nitrogen into the atmosphere.

Nanotech Age — This era is characterized by molecular construction, molecule-sized machines, and completely automatic production.

Nemesis — The culprit in the periodic mass extinctions (every 25 million years or so). Identity unknown, the two prime suspects are: Meteors (caused by a dark star orbiting our Sun) and Explosive Upwellings.

Nitrogen (N_2) — A gas composed of two nitrogen atoms. It is a heavy, stable gas comprising 80% of Earth's atmosphere.

Noosphere — "The sphere of mind" which includes society and culture.

Order — The classification of life under Class. The major orders of mammals are rodents, felines, canines, ruminants, primates and cetaceans.

Organism — An independent unit of life. All plants, animals and microbes are organisms.

Oxygen (O$_2$) — A gas composed of two oxygen atoms. This is used by organisms when they respirate.

Oxygenator — A SimEarth tool that converts carbon dioxide to oxygen.

Photosynthesis — A process that uses light to create energy-storing chemicals such as sugar. Oxygen is a byproduct of photosynthesis.

Plant — An organism that uses photosynthesis to feed itself.

Plate — A solid piece of the Earth's crust being pushed about by flowing mantle.

Plate Tectonics — Theory that the Earth's crust is formed of mobile plates sliding across the mantle. Even the ocean bottoms consist of plates.

Phylum — The classification of life under Kingdom. The major animal phylums are chordates, arthropods and invertebrates. See Class.

Phytomass — The total dry weight of all plant material on a planet.

Planet — An astral body that orbits a sun.

Planetesimal — An small planet. Small usually means moon-sized or less.

Prokaryote — Primitive single-cell microbes with no nucleus.

Radiate — The class of invertebrates including jellyfish and starfish.

Sapient — An intelligent, tool-using organism.

Stone Age — This era is characterized by stone tools, domestication, fire, and cultivation.

Surface Albedo — In SimEarth this refers to the albedo of your planetary surface.

Swamp — Also known as tropical grasslands. This biome is composed of plants and animals that thrive in slow shallow water and on muddy shorelines.

Terraform — The process of modifying an entire planet for a particular purpose.

Trichordate — A SimEarth term for an order of radiates with three radiating spines.

Tundra — This biome is designed to survive periodic arctic conditions and year-round cold weather.

Upwelling — When two plates pull apart, lava will flow up between them forming small rises like the Mid-Atlantic Ridge. See Plate Tectonics.

Vaporator — A SimEarth tool that stimulates global plant growth.

Volcano — When a Hot Spot is over a thin section of crust, a volcano can erupt. Volcanos spew lava and ash over an area, often forming new cone-shaped mountains.

Water Vapor (H$_2$O) — Water can be a gas with one oxygen atom and two hydrogen atoms.

Zoomass — The total dry weight of all animal material on a planet.

SIMEARTH INDEX

PLANET SPECIFICATION SHEET

MERCURY

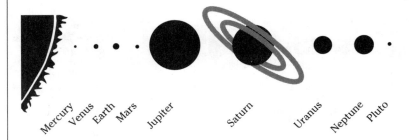

Mercury Venus Earth Mars Jupiter Saturn Uranus Neptune Pluto

Year (Earth days) ———————————87.97
Day (Earth hours) ————————————59
Diameter (km) ————————————4880
Diameter (miles)———————————3032
Density (water = 1) ————————————5.5
Moons ——————————————————0
Surface Gravity (Earth = 1)———————.38
Mass (x10,000,000,000,000 Gigatons) ———.332
Distance from Sun (Million km) ————————57.9
Distance from the Sun (Million miles) ——35.99
Orbital Velocity (km/sec) ——————————— 47.73

VENUS

PLANET SPECIFICATION SHEET

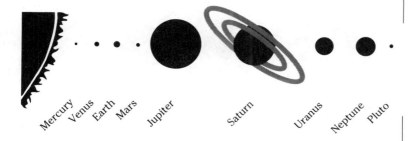

Mercury Venus Earth Mars Jupiter Saturn Uranus Neptune Pluto

Year (Earth days)	224.7
Day (Earth days)	243
Diameter (km)	12100
Diameter (miles)	7523
Average Temperature (°C)	477
Density (water = 1)	5.24
Moons	0
Surface Gravity (Earth = 1)	.9
Mass (x10,000,000,000,000 Gigatons)	4.89
Axial Tilt	177.3
Volume (Earth = 1)	.88
Distance from Sun (Million km)	108.2
Distance from the Sun (Million miles)	67.24
Orbital Velocity (km/sec)	35

PLANET
SPECIFICATION
SHEET

EARTH

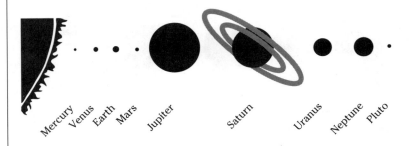

Mercury Venus Earth Mars Jupiter Saturn Uranus Neptune Pluto

Year (Earth days) ———————————365.26
Day (Earth hours) ———————————23h 56m
Diameter (km)—————————————12754
Diameter (miles)————————————7926
Average Temperature (°C) ——————————13
Density (water = 1) ————————————5.52
Moons ——————————————————1
Surface Gravity (Earth = 1) ————————1
Mass (x10,000,000,000,000 Gigatons) ———6.04
Axial Tilt ——————————————————23.45
Volume (Earth = 1) ———————————1
Distance from Sun (Million km) ————149.6
Distance from the Sun (Million miles) ———93
Orbital Velocity (km/sec) ———————29.8

MARS

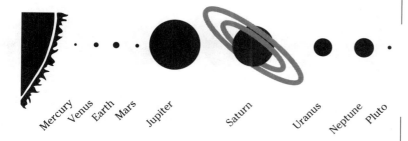

Mercury Venus Earth Mars Jupiter Saturn Uranus Neptune Pluto

Year (Earth days) ———————————687
Day (Earth hours) ———————————24h 37m
Diameter (km) ———————————6796
Diameter (miles)———————————4220
Average Temperature (°C) ——————— –53
Density (water = 1) ———————————3.94
Moons ———————————2
Surface Gravity (Earth = 1)———————.38
Mass (x10,000,000,000,000 Gigatons) ———.642
Axial Tilt ———————————25.19
Volume (Earth = 1)———————————.15
Distance from Sun (Million km) ———————227.9
Distance from the Sun (Million miles) ——141.73
Orbital Velocity (km/sec) ———————————24.1

PLANET
SPECIFICATION
SHEET

JUPITER

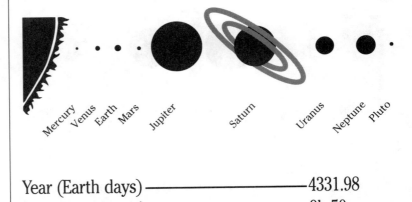

Mercury   Venus   Earth   Mars   Jupiter   Saturn   Uranus   Neptune   Pluto

Year (Earth days) ————————————4331.98
Day (Earth hours) ————————————9h 50m
Diameter (km)————————————————142800
Diameter (miles)———————————————88750
Density (water = 1) ——————————————1.3
Moons ————————————————————16
Surface Gravity (Earth = 1)————————2.87
Mass (x10,000,000,000,000 Gigatons) ———1920
Distance from Sun (Million km) —————778.7
Distance from the Sun (Million miles) ——483.88
Orbital Velocity (km/sec) ————————12.73

SATURN

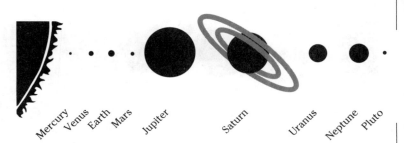

Mercury Venus Earth Mars Jupiter Saturn Uranus Neptune Pluto

Year (Earth days) —————————— 10760.56
Day (Earth hours) —————————— 10h 14m
Diameter (km)————————————— 120020
Diameter (miles) ————————————— 74580
Density (water = 1) ————————————— 0.7
Moons —————————————————— 17
Surface Gravity (Earth = 1)———————— 1.32
Mass (x10,000,000,000,000 Gigatons) ———— 575
Distance from Sun (Million km) ————— 1427.7
Distance from the Sun (Million miles) —— 887.13
Orbital Velocity (km/sec) ———————— 9.45

PLANET SPECIFICATION SHEET

URANUS

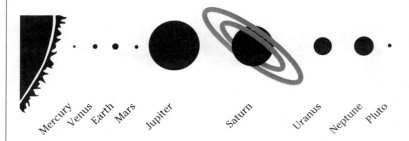

Mercury   Venus   Earth   Mars   Jupiter   Saturn   Uranus   Neptune   Pluto

Year (Earth days) ——————————30685.49
Day (Earth hours) ——————————10h 49m
Diameter (km)————————————50900
Diameter (miles) ————————————31600
Density (water = 1) ——————————1.3
Moons ——————————————————5
Surface Gravity (Earth = 1)——————0.93
Mass (x10,000,000,000,000 Gigatons) ———88.2
Distance from Sun (Million km) ————2870.5
Distance from the Sun (Million miles) ——1783.7
Orbital Velocity (km/sec) ————————6.36

NEPTUNE

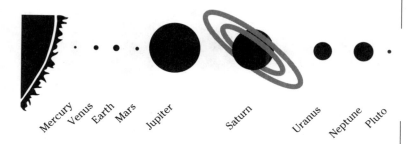

Mercury Venus Earth Mars Jupiter Saturn Uranus Neptune Pluto

Year (Earth days) ——————————60191.2
Day (Earth hours) ——————————15h 48m
Diameter (km)————————————48600
Diameter (miles)————————————30200
Density (water = 1) ————————————1.8
Moons ——————————————————3
Surface Gravity (Earth = 1)————————1.23
Mass (x10,000,000,000,000 Gigatons)———103.89
Distance from Sun (Million km) ————4498.8
Distance from the Sun (Million miles) ——2795.5
Orbital Velocity (km/sec) ————————4.77

PLANET SPECIFICATION SHEET

PLUTO

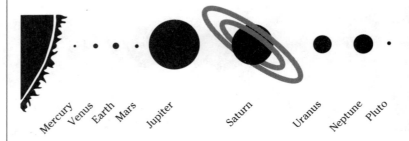

Mercury   Venus   Earth   Mars   Jupiter   Saturn   Uranus   Neptune   Pluto

Year (Earth days) —————————90474.9
Day (Earth hours) —————————159h 19m
Diameter (km) ——————————2400
Diameter (miles) —————————1500
Density (water = 1)————————0.7(?)
Moons ——————————————1
Surface Gravity (Earth = 1) ————0.03(?)
Mass (x10,000,000,000,000 Gigatons) ———.06
Distance from Sun (Million km) ———5902.8
Distance from the Sun (Million miles) ——3667.9
Orbital Velocity (km/sec) —————<4.77